What You Really Need to Know Before You Go Thailand (Travel Guide)

Essential Tips, Local Culture, and Must-See Spots for an Unforgettable Experience.

Jose K. Solomon

Copyright © 2024 by Jose K. Solomon

Disclaimer

This travel guide provides information and suggestions to help travelers plan their visit to New York City. While every effort has been made to ensure the accuracy and reliability of the content at the time of publication, changes in business hours, entry fees, services, and local laws may occur. The author and publisher are not responsible for any losses, injuries, or inconveniences sustained by readers as a result of the information presented in this book.

The mention of specific companies, products, or services does not imply endorsement or recommendation by the author or publisher. Readers should conduct their own research and seek professional advice where necessary.

TABLE OF CONTENTS

INTRODUCTION

Thailand is a land of contrast and color, a place where ancient traditions meet modern living, and lush landscapes blend with bustling cityscapes. This guide is designed to help you navigate through Thailand's rich offerings, from the gleaming temples and cultural festivals to the vibrant street markets and serene islands.

Understanding Thailand is key to enjoying your visit. The country is divided into several regions, each with its own distinct characteristics and attractions. The bustling city of Bangkok offers a dynamic atmosphere with its incredible shopping districts and nightlife. The northern part of Thailand, with Chiang Mai at its heart, invites travelers with its cooler climates, mountainous landscapes, and rich history of Lanna culture. The northeast, known as Isan, is less traveled but no less fascinating, offering ancient Khmer ruins and vibrant festivals. Down south, the beaches of Phuket and Krabi draw sun-seekers from around the world with their stunning coastlines and blue waters.

In this guide, you will find detailed information that will help you plan your travels, from tips on the best times to visit to avoid the rainy season, to advice on how to get around using local transportation like tuk-tuks and motorbike taxis. You'll also learn how to interact with locals respectfully, understanding important customs and traditions to ensure your interactions are always courteous and welcomed.

Dining in Thailand is an adventure in itself, known globally for its bold flavors and aromatic dishes. Here, you will discover where to find the most authentic Thai food, from street vendors serving up Pad Thai and Som Tum to fine dining restaurants offering curated menus of local dishes.

For those looking to explore beyond the typical tourist paths, this guide also highlights some hidden gems and less-visited locales that offer unique experiences, from quiet beach retreats to local markets teeming with crafts and produce.

With every chapter, you'll gain more insight into how to make the most of your trip to Thailand, ensuring it is filled with enjoyment, discovery, and a deeper understanding of this beautiful country's heart and soul. Turn the page to start crafting an itinerary that brings you face to face with the unforgettable wonders of Thailand.

CHAPTER 1

DISCOVERING THAILAND

Thailand is a vibrant tapestry of history, culture, and landscapes that promises to enchant every traveler who steps onto its soil. As someone who has traversed its bustling city streets and serene countryside, I'm excited to share a glimpse into what makes Thailand a truly unique destination.

In the chapters that follow, we'll dive into the rich history of Thailand, a saga woven with the threads of ancient civilizations, royal dynasties, and transformative events that have shaped the nation into what it is today. From the ruins of Ayutthaya to the grandeur of the Grand Palace in Bangkok, the past is alive here, and each site tells a story worth discovering.

We'll also explore Thailand's geography, a diverse palette that ranges from lush, rolling hills in the north to pristine beaches that fringe the southern coasts. This geographical diversity not only shapes the climate and natural beauty of Thailand but also influences the local lifestyles, cuisines, and traditions that vary dramatically from region to region.

Understanding cultural norms and etiquette is crucial for any traveler, and in Thailand, the grace with which the locals navigate their social interactions is something to behold. We'll cover the essential dos and don'ts that will help you respect and embrace Thai customs, from the wai, a traditional greeting involving a slight bow with palms pressed together, to navigating the nuances of dining etiquette.

Throughout this guide, I aim to equip you with knowledge and insights that will enhance your journey, making each moment in Thailand as fulfilling as it can be. Whether you're a seasoned traveler or a curious explorer, this guide will serve as your gateway to truly understanding and appreciating this incredible country. Join me in unraveling the enchanting stories and experiences that Thailand has to offer.

The Rich Tapestry of Thai History

Thailand's history is a rich, colorful mosaic, steeped in tradition and filled with epochs of transformative change that have contributed to the nation's identity today. My journey through its historical landscapes was nothing short of a step back in time, each corner unfolding stories that have shaped the vibrant culture of this country.

Let me share with you the deep-seated history of Thailand, beginning with its early civilizations. The roots of Thai history can be traced back to the kingdoms of Sukhothai and Ayutthaya, where the foundations of Thai culture, religion, and monarchy were laid. As I walked through the historical park in Sukhothai, it was easy to imagine the grandeur of what was once the cradle of Thai civilization. The remnants of beautiful, detailed statues and the still-intact structures speak volumes about the creativity and architectural ingenuity of the Thais during the 13th century.

Moving forward in time, the Ayutthaya period, which succeeded Sukhothai, marked a significant era where trade with foreign nations brought prosperity and a rich diversity of influences to Thai culture. The ruins of Ayutthaya, with their intricate carvings and robust structures, are a testament to the kingdom's might and its central role in regional trade. Standing amongst these ruins, I felt a profound connection to the past, a reminder of the resilience of the Thai people.

The historical narrative of Thailand is also marked by the era of Rattanakosin, beginning in the late 18th century when Bangkok was established as the capital. This period is renowned for its artistic and cultural renaissance. As I meandered through the bustling streets of Bangkok, the magnificent temples and palaces such as the Grand Palace and Wat Phra Kaew served as vivid illustrations of this golden age. The intricate detail and symbolic meanings embedded in these structures are a showcase of Thai craftsmanship and religious devotion.

Understanding Thai history also involves recognizing the challenges it faced. From colonial pressures to internal reforms, Thailand navigated through turbulent times without being colonized—a unique aspect of its history that has instilled a strong sense of national pride among Thais. This resilience is palpable as you talk to local people, whose ancestors lived through these dynamic times.

My travels through Thailand have not only been a journey through its landscapes but also a profound educational experience into its historical depth. The stories embedded in its ancient cities, the legacy of its kingdoms, and the enduring spirit of its people make Thailand's history not just a series of past events, but a continuous narrative that every visitor can learn from and be inspired by. As we explore Thailand, understanding this history enriches our travels, making every sight more meaningful and every encounter more enriching.

An Overview of Thailand's Geography

Exploring the geography of Thailand is like opening a vibrant atlas filled with landscapes so diverse that every region presents a new chapter. From my travels, I've gathered a deep appreciation for this country's rich tapestry of geography, which ranges from lush jungles and expansive rice fields to dramatic coastlines and bustling cities.

Thailand is uniquely positioned in Southeast Asia, bordered by Myanmar to the northwest, Laos to the northeast, Cambodia to the southeast, and Malaysia to the south. This strategic location has made it a crossroads for various cultures, influences, and, importantly, a diverse range of ecosystems. The variety in terrain and climate across the country is profound, and understanding this geography helps to appreciate how it shapes the local lifestyles and cultures.

In the north, the geography is dominated by the rugged highlands, a continuation of the mountain chains from Myanmar. The mountains here are more than just a breathtaking backdrop; they are integral to the community, with villages and towns nestled in valleys that boast a cooler climate than the sweltering plains below. Trekking through the hills of Chiang Mai, I was enveloped in mists and the fresh, crisp air that contrasts sharply with the humidity of other regions. The highlands are also the source of Thailand's major rivers, including the mighty Chao Phraya that flows southward to Bangkok, feeding the fertile plains that have historically been the rice bowl of Asia.

Heading southwards, the central plains, including the expansive area around Bangkok, are often referred to as the heartland of Thailand. This region is characterized by flat, low-lying lands that are occasionally interrupted by limestone hills. The central plains are crucial for agriculture, particularly rice cultivation, which is evident in the endless green paddies that stretch towards the horizon, particularly during the rainy season. The Chao Phraya River and its tributaries crisscross these plains, creating a network of waterways that have shaped the economic and cultural life of the country.

The eastern part of Thailand, while similar to the central plains, is more notable for its fruit production. As I ventured through provinces like Chanthaburi, I was delighted by the abundance of tropical fruits like durian, rambutan, and mangosteen, which thrive in the region's rich, volcanic soil.

Down south, Thailand extends into the narrow Kra Isthmus before broadening out into the Malay Peninsula. Here, the geography is dramatically different again, with stunning coastlines on both the Gulf of Thailand and the Andaman Sea. The southern region is renowned for its idyllic islands and beaches that attract visitors from around the world. Places like Phuket and Krabi are not just holiday spots but also key points in understanding Thailand's geographical diversity.

Each region of Thailand tells a story through its geography, from the high northern mountains descending through the central plains to the tropical islands in the south. Traveling through these landscapes has not only shown me the physical beauty of Thailand but has also provided insights into how geography influences daily life, from the foods people grow to the traditional homes that blend with the natural environment. This deep connection with the land is something that stays with you long after the journey ends, leaving a lasting impression of Thailand's diverse geographical tapestry.

Cultural Norms and Etiquette

Navigating the cultural norms and etiquette in Thailand is an essential aspect of truly understanding and appreciating this beautiful country. During my travels here, I quickly learned that the Thai people place a high value on politeness and respect, which is woven deeply into their social fabric.

One of the first and most profound customs I encountered in Thailand is the 'wai.' This traditional Thai greeting involves a slight bow, with the palms pressed together in a prayer-like fashion. It is not just a sign of greeting but also of respect and gratitude. The position of the hands and the depth of the bow vary depending on the social status or age of the person you are greeting. It's a beautiful, serene gesture that I found quite meaningful.

Another crucial aspect of Thai culture is the concept of 'face.' Maintaining one's dignity and helping others to 'save face' by not embarrassing or confronting them publicly is of utmost importance. This cultural nuance affects everything from casual conversations to business meetings. I learned to be more mindful of how my words and actions might affect not just the outcome of a discussion but the comfort and self-esteem of the people involved.

Respect for the monarchy is also deeply ingrained in Thai society. Criticism or disrespect towards the royal family is not only frowned upon but is also illegal under Thai law. Observing this reverence firsthand during ceremonies and national holidays, I felt the deep loyalty and veneration that Thais hold towards their monarchy.

Religion plays a pivotal role in daily Thai life, with the majority of Thais being Buddhist. Visiting the myriad temples, I was struck by the calm and devotion that permeates these sacred spaces. Dressing modestly is required; shoulders and knees must be covered, and shoes removed before entering temple buildings. Watching devotees offer food to monks in the early morning was a poignant reminder of the communal support and respect for the monastic community.

Dining etiquette in Thailand also has its particularities. For instance, the fork and spoon are the usual utensils, with the fork used to push food onto the spoon, which is the primary utensil brought to the mouth. Chopsticks are generally used only for noodle dishes. Sharing meals is common, and it's considered polite to wait for the eldest at the table to start eating first.

One of my favorite memories is participating in the Songkran festival, the Thai New Year, where respect for elders is beautifully expressed through the ritual of pouring water over their hands. It's also a time for playful water throwing, which speaks to another essential aspect of Thai culture: 'sanuk,' or the importance of deriving pleasure and enjoyment from every activity.

Understanding and embracing these cultural norms and etiquette has not only enriched my experience in Thailand but has also allowed me to connect with locals in a more meaningful, respectful way. The warmth and friendliness of Thai people make it easy to fall in love with this country, and knowing how to navigate these cultural nuances makes the journey even more rewarding.

CHAPTER 2

TRAVEL ESSENTIALS

Before setting off on my own Thai adventure, I realized how essential it was to be well-prepared. Knowing what to pack, when to visit, and understanding the local customs can make all the difference in experiencing Thailand—not just as a tourist, but as a welcomed guest. In this chapter, we'll explore the key essentials every traveler should consider to make their journey smooth and memorable.

We'll start by figuring out the best time to visit. Thailand's weather varies dramatically from season to season, and each brings its own set of festivities. Whether you're aiming to participate in the cool, celebratory atmosphere of the Loy Krathong Festival or enjoy the tropical beaches in their prime, knowing the right season for your travels is crucial.

Then, we'll navigate through the logistics of entering the country. The visa requirements for Thailand have nuances depending on where you're coming from, and the length of your stay. I'll share some firsthand tips on how to ensure your paperwork is as in order as your itinerary.

Health and safety are not to be overlooked. From necessary vaccinations to securing travel insurance, I'll provide insights into how to travel with peace of mind. No one wants to encounter a medical mishap away from home without preparation.

Lastly, we'll cover some essential Thai phrases. Communicating with locals in their language can enrich your experience, helping you connect with the culture in a more meaningful way. A simple 'Sawasdee' (hello) with a smile can open doors to genuine interactions.

By the end of this chapter, you'll feel equipped and ready to embark on your Thai journey with confidence, ensuring every moment spent in this stunning country is nothing short of incredible.

Best Travel Seasons: Weather and Festivities

Choosing when to visit Thailand is almost as important as deciding where to go within the country. From my own experiences and what I've gathered from many friendly locals, timing your visit can dramatically affect not just the weather you'll encounter, but also the cultural festivities you might experience.

Thailand's climate is tropical, marked by three main seasons. First, there's the hot season, running from March through June. During these months, temperatures can soar above 40 degrees Celsius (104 degrees Fahrenheit) in some areas, particularly in and around Bangkok. While it might seem daunting, the hot season has its perks, especially for visiting the spectacular beaches of the southern islands where breezes make the heat bearable.

Then comes the rainy season, from July to October. The monsoon rains can be unpredictable, but they often arrive in brief, heavy downpours, typically in the afternoon, leaving the rest of the day warm and pleasantly washed. This season paints the landscapes with lush greenery, and the waterfalls in the northern mountains are at their most majestic. Traveling during this time also means fewer tourists and lower prices, with the scenery at its peak of tropical lushness.

The cool season, from November to February, is arguably the best time to visit. The weather is milder, making it ideal for exploring cultural sites in the north like Chiang Mai or the historical parks in Sukhothai and Ayutthaya without the exhausting heat. It's also during this season that Thailand bursts into a myriad of festivals. The Loy Krathong Festival in November is particularly magical; watching thousands of lanterns float into the night sky is an unforgettable sight. Similarly, the Thai New Year, or Songkran, in April is an exhilarating water festival where everyone, young and old, joins in the playful splashing of water, celebrating in a spirit of joy and renewal.

Having experienced these seasons myself, I found that each offers a unique perspective of Thailand. Whether you're looking to soak in the sun on palm-fringed beaches, trek through verdant jungles, or immerse yourself in the bustling city life, choosing the right season can enhance your experience, allowing you to engage deeply with both the place and its people. Understanding these patterns also helps in packing the right things—whether it's rain gear for the monsoon months or extra sunscreen for the scorching summer days.

In planning your trip, consider not just the places you wish to explore but also the seasonal contexts that might define your travel experience. Thailand is vibrant and full of life year-round, but finding your perfect moment to visit can make your journey even more special.

Preparing for Your Trip: Visa and Entry Requirements

Planning a trip to Thailand involves not just packing your bags and booking flights, but also understanding the visa and entry requirements. During my preparations for Thailand, navigating through the visa process was a crucial step that set the stage for a smooth travel experience. Let me share some insights on what to expect and how to prepare effectively.

Thailand's visa policy is quite welcoming, allowing tourists from numerous countries to enter without a visa for short stays, typically up to 30 days, when arriving by air. However, if you plan to stay longer, or if you're arriving by land, the rules might differ. For instance, land entries from neighboring countries might limit you to just 15 days without a visa. It's important to check the most current policies from official resources or the Thai embassy in your country before making travel plans.

For those needing a visa for longer visits, Thailand offers several types, including tourist visas that are valid for 60 days and can be extended for another 30 days once you are in the country. Applying for a tourist visa usually involves submitting your application to a Thai consulate or embassy, along with your passport, proof of onward travel, and proof of sufficient funds. I found that having all my documents organized beforehand made the process smoother and quicker.

Another essential step in preparing for your trip to Thailand is understanding the entry requirements related to health. For instance, while Thailand does not generally require proof of vaccinations unless you're coming from a yellow fever-endemic area, it's wise to be up-to-date with routine shots like tetanus and hepatitis A and B, especially if you plan to explore rural areas.

During the COVID-19 pandemic, additional health documentation such as proof of vaccination or negative tests was required. While many of these requirements have been relaxed, it's crucial to verify the latest health and safety guidelines close to your departure date. Changes can happen rapidly, and being informed will help avoid any last-minute surprises.

Lastly, ensure your passport has at least six months of validity from the date of entry into Thailand, as this is a standard requirement for many countries. Also, having a few passport photos handy can save time if you need to apply for a visa extension or other permits during your stay.

In my experience, taking the time to understand these entry nuances not only eased my mind but also prevented potential hurdles that could disrupt an exciting adventure in Thailand. Remember, a little preparation goes a long way toward ensuring your visit is nothing short of spectacular.

Health and Safety: Vaccinations and Travel Insurance

Preparing for health and safety is as crucial as packing your essentials when planning a trip to Thailand. On my own journey, ensuring I was well-informed about vaccinations and travel insurance was a top priority that helped make my trip worry-free and secure.

Firstly, vaccinations are a key consideration when traveling to any new country, and Thailand is no exception. Based on my health provider's advice, I made sure to be up to date on routine vaccines such as measles-mumps-rubella (MMR), diphtheria-tetanus-pertussis, varicella (chickenpox), polio, and your yearly flu shot. Additionally, vaccinations for hepatitis A and typhoid are highly recommended for most travelers to Thailand because you can contract these diseases through contaminated food or water, regardless of where you are staying.

For those venturing into more rural areas or planning an extended stay, vaccines for hepatitis B and Japanese encephalitis might also be advised. Hepatitis B can be contracted through contact with blood or other bodily fluids, and Japanese encephalitis from mosquito bites. Malaria prophylaxis might also be considered if you're planning to visit rural regions, especially near the borders with Cambodia, Laos, and Myanmar. My doctor recommended I carry mosquito repellent and sleep under a mosquito net in those areas, which I found immensely helpful.

Travel insurance is another essential that shouldn't be overlooked. Before heading to Thailand, I ensured my policy covered medical expenses, as the cost of treatment can be high, and the last thing you want is to be stranded without help in case of a medical emergency. Many policies also cover trip cancellations, lost luggage, and other unforeseen issues that could arise. This was comforting, as it meant I could recover some costs if my plans were disrupted by situations beyond my control.

I recall meeting a fellow traveler who had an accident while riding a motorbike in Chiang Mai and had to seek extensive medical care. Thanks to their travel insurance, they were able to receive excellent care at a private hospital without the stress of a hefty bill. This incident was a practical reminder of why having robust insurance is indispensable.

Finally, while the excitement of travel can be all-consuming, it's vital to heed local health advisories and safety guidelines. During my stay, I regularly checked updates on local health conditions and ensured I followed the recommended precautions, such as drinking bottled or purified water and avoiding street food that didn't look fresh.

Navigating health and safety precautions with thorough preparation not only protected me but also ensured that my travel experience was as smooth and enjoyable as possible. Taking these steps allowed me to focus more on the incredible sights and experiences Thailand had to offer, with the peace of mind that I was well-prepared for any health-related issues that could arise.

Glossary of Essential Thai Phrases

When I first arrived in Thailand, I quickly realized that learning a few key phrases in Thai could go a long way in enhancing my travel experience. Communicating, even minimally, in the local language not only eased daily interactions but also brought smiles and appreciative nods from locals, enriching my journey with genuine connections. Here's a handy glossary of essential Thai phrases that I found invaluable during my travels, which I'm eager to share to help smooth your path as you explore the enchanting landscapes and vibrant cities of Thailand.

Sawasdee (khrap/ka) - สวัสดี (ครับ/ค่ะ): This is the universal Thai greeting and probably the most important word to know. Say "Sawasdee khrap" if you are male and "Sawasdee ka" if you are female. This small effort in greeting someone in their local language brings about a friendly atmosphere instantly.

Khob khun (khrap/ka) - ขอบคุณ (ครับ/ค่ะ): Thank you. Another critical phrase to express gratitude. Again, end with "khrap" if you are a man and "ka" if you are a woman, which is polite and shows respect.

Chai (Yes) / Mai (No) - ใช่ / ไม่: These basic affirmatives are simple yet powerful. Whether you're agreeing to a ride, confirming a meal choice, or simply acknowledging a question, these words will be a part of your daily vocabulary in Thailand.

Mai pen rai - ไม่เป็นไร: Often translated as 'it's okay' or 'no problem,' this phrase is the quintessential Thai expression of letting go and one of the most commonly used phrases. It reflects the Thai way of life—relaxed and easy-going. When someone apologizes to you, responding with "Mai pen rai" will put them at ease.

Tao rai? - เท่าไร?: How much? This question is crucial in markets or when taking tuk-tuks and taxis. Knowing how to ask this helps you get into bargaining conversations, which are a part of the shopping experience in Thailand.

Hong nam yoo tee nai? - ห้องน้ำอยู่ที่ไหน?: Where is the bathroom? A practical question that is always useful to know in any language.

Aroy - อร่อย: Delicious. Thai food is world-renowned, and you'll likely use this word often. Complimenting a chef or a street food vendor with this word after a meal can be very pleasing to hear.

Khor tort - ขอโทษ: Excuse me or sorry. Whether you're navigating through crowded streets, catching someone's attention, or apologizing, this phrase is handy to clear the way or show politeness.

Phom dong gaan long thang nee - ผม/ดิฉัน ต้องการลงที่นี่: I want to get off here. Useful when you're traveling by bus or taxi and need to tell the driver where you need to stop.

Kee moh? - คีม่อ: How much? This is specifically useful when discussing prices in markets or stores.

Mastering these phrases didn't just make my day-to-day activities smoother but also opened up a new dimension of interaction that was beyond the usual tourist experience. People appreciated my efforts to speak their language, and it often led to heartwarming exchanges, helpful tips from locals, and even invitations to local gatherings. Knowing these essential Thai phrases truly enriched my travel experience, making my adventures in Thailand far more meaningful and enjoyable.

CHAPTER 3

GETTING THERE

Setting foot in Thailand, with its tapestry of colors, landscapes, and cultural richness, is a dream for many travelers, including myself. Navigating your arrival and entry into Thailand is your first step into a world of adventure, and understanding the best ways to get there can make all the difference in starting your trip smoothly. In this chapter, I'll share essential insights on the practical aspects of traveling to this vibrant country.

First, we'll delve into navigating air travel, highlighting key airports across Thailand. From the bustling Suvarnabhumi Airport in Bangkok to the more tranquil Chiang Mai International Airport in the north, knowing which airport to fly into can save you time and align better with your travel itinerary. I'll also share some booking tips that have helped me snag great deals and convenient flights, which are invaluable for budget-savvy travelers and those looking to make the most of their time in Thailand.

For those with a sense of adventure or coming from nearby countries, sea and land entries offer a fascinating alternative to air travel. We'll explore the main border crossings and ferry services, providing a scenic entry into the kingdom. Whether you're crossing over from Laos into the lush northern regions of Thailand or catching a ferry from

Malaysia to the southern Thai beaches, each route offers its own unique charm and challenges.

Lastly, choosing the right travel insurance is crucial. This section will guide you through selecting a policy that covers everything from medical emergencies to trip cancellations. Having had to use my travel insurance during a minor mishap in Phuket, I can't stress enough how vital it is to be covered. It not only gives you peace of mind but also ensures that unforeseen events don't derail your travel plans.

By the end of this chapter, you'll be well-equipped with the knowledge to make your journey to Thailand not just a possibility, but a delightful certainty, filled with anticipation for the experiences that await. So, let's prepare to embark on this exciting venture together, with all the practical information you'll need to begin your Thai adventure.

Navigating Air Travel: Key Airports and Booking Tips

Flying into Thailand offers a glimpse into the efficiency and charm that the country extends to visitors right from their first touchpoint—its airports. My own travels through Thailand began with a touchdown at Bangkok's Suvarnabhumi Airport, one of Southeast Asia's busiest hubs. The beauty of flying into Thailand is that you're not just funneled through a generic terminal but rather welcomed by spaces that blend modern amenities with touches of Thai culture.

Suvarnabhumi Airport in Bangkok, along with Don Mueang International Airport, serves as the primary gateways for international travelers. Suvarnabhumi is a hub for most major international airlines and a dazzling example of contemporary airport architecture. If you're flying from within Asia or on low-cost carriers, Don Mueang might very well be where you'll disembark. Both airports are equipped with extensive visitor services, from on-site hotels to quick city links, making them not just transit points but part of your travel experience.

For those venturing to the northern reaches of Thailand, Chiang Mai International Airport offers a warm welcome. Less overwhelming than its Bangkok counterparts, it provides a friendly introduction to the slower pace of life you can expect in the north. Here, the airport itself is close to city centers, which means you could be sipping a local coffee or walking through a night market within an hour of grabbing your bags.

Phuket International Airport is the gateway to the south's island paradises. Flying here directly can save you a considerable amount of travel time and offers the quickest route to the sandy shores and blue waters of Thai beaches. Once at the airport, the transition from the plane to beach can be surprisingly quick, provided you've timed your flights to dodge the major tourist rushes.

When booking flights to Thailand, my top tip is to look for deals during the shoulder seasons—just before and after the high tourist seasons. Prices tend to drop yet the weather remains quite pleasant. Websites and apps that track flight prices can alert you to a sudden drop in fares, making sure you get the best deal possible.

Another tip is to consider flying mid-week. Not only are flights often cheaper, but airports are less crowded, allowing for a smoother arrival process. Once you've booked your flight, ensure you've read up on the airport services. For example, Suvarnabhumi offers sleep pods and showers, perfect for a refreshing break if you have a layover or arrive after a long flight.

At each of these airports, you'll find that Thai hospitality begins to shine through. Whether it's through a local meal at an airport eatery or a Thai massage at an airport spa, your journey can begin on a high note right from arrival.

Navigating air travel in Thailand is not just about moving from point A to point B; it's about the experiences along the way. From the moment you land, the country offers opportunities to immerse yourself in its culture, from traditional Thai meals at airport restaurants to local handicrafts sold at airport shops. These airports don't just serve as entry points; they are part of your Thai adventure, setting the tone for a memorable visit. By managing your travel logistics smartly and embracing these hubs of activity, you ensure your trip is stress-free and filled with delightful experiences from the get-go.

Sea and Land Entry: Borders, Ferries, and Crossings

Exploring Thailand doesn't always mean flying directly into its bustling airports. Many travelers, myself included, find charm and adventure in entering Thailand by sea and land. This route not only unveils some scenic views and unique experiences but also connects you to the essence of travel by merging journeys through various landscapes and cultural exchanges at border points.

Sea Entry: For those arriving from nearby countries, or who simply prefer the scenic route, entering Thailand by sea is an enchanting option. Numerous ferries connect Thailand to its neighboring countries, including Malaysia and Indonesia. One of the most popular sea routes is from Langkawi to Satun in southern Thailand. The ferry ride offers breathtaking views of the Andaman Sea and leads you directly into some of Thailand's famed southern provinces, known for their pristine beaches and rich marine life. Arriving by sea gives you the unique advantage of stepping ashore right into coastal towns where seafood is fresh and beaches are less crowded.

Land Crossings: Thailand shares borders with Myanmar, Laos, Cambodia, and Malaysia, each offering several crossing points that are well-traveled by locals and tourists alike. One memorable crossing I experienced was at the Aranyaprathet border from Cambodia into Thailand. The journey through these land crossings is an eye-opener into the daily lives of locals—marketplaces bustling with activity, street food vendors offering local delicacies, and the vibrant culture that seeps through every interaction. Many travelers use these crossings to extend their Southeast Asian tour, making Thailand a part of a larger exploration, which adds layers to their travel stories.

Border Crossings: Navigating through these borders requires some preparation. Ensuring you have the correct visa is crucial, as visa requirements can vary based on your nationality and the specific border you choose to cross. I found that keeping multiple photocopies of my passport and visa helped speed up the process at checkpoints. It's also useful to carry some local currency, as border areas might not readily accept credit cards or foreign currency.

Making the Experience Memorable: Beyond the practicalities, entering Thailand by land or sea can enrich your travel experience. For instance, taking a slow boat down the Mekong River into Thailand from Laos allows you to witness the tranquil rural landscapes and traditional riverine life, a stark contrast to the bustling city vibes you'll find in urban Thailand. Similarly, crossing by land from

Malaysia lets you experience the gradual change in culture, cuisine, and architecture—an evolution from one nation to another.

Moreover, these entry points often lead to lesser-known regions that are rich in culture and history. The towns near borders offer unique shopping experiences, where local crafts and goods are available at prices significantly lower than in major tourist spots. They also provide a glimpse into the harmonious blend of cultures, especially in areas where communities from both sides of the border mingle.

Entering Thailand by sea or land isn't merely about stepping from one country to another; it's about the stories that unfold along the way, the people you meet, and the landscapes that gradually shift before your eyes. It's a reminder that sometimes, the journey itself can be as enriching as the destination. For those looking to dive deeper into the Thai experience, considering these alternative routes can open up a whole new dimension of adventure and cultural immersion.

Choosing Your Travel Insurance: What to Look For

Choosing the right travel insurance for a trip to Thailand is a pivotal step in your travel preparations, one that I regard with the utmost importance based on my own experiences. Ensuring you have adequate coverage can transform potential mishaps into mere hiccups along the road of your adventure, allowing you to enjoy the countless experiences Thailand has to offer without undue worry.

When selecting travel insurance, the first thing to look for is comprehensive medical coverage. Medical treatment in Thailand can be excellent in major cities like Bangkok or Chiang Mai, where private hospitals offer world-class care. However, these can be costly without insurance, especially if complex procedures or medical evacuation is needed. It's wise to ensure your policy covers both, as well as transportation to the nearest hospital of international standard, should you find yourself in more remote areas.

Another essential feature is coverage for trip interruptions or cancellations. Thailand is a tropical paradise but also prone to seasonal weather like monsoons, which can disrupt travel plans. During one of my trips, a sudden storm meant a delayed flight, leading to an unexpected overnight stay in Phuket. My travel insurance covered the cost of accommodation and meals during the delay, which eased what could have been a stressful situation.

Additionally, if you're planning to indulge in activities such as scuba diving in Ko Tao, motorbiking across the northern mountains, or even ziplining in Chiang Rai, you'll want to check that your insurance covers accidents resulting from these activities. Many standard policies exclude "adventure" sports unless specific coverage is requested, so it's crucial to tailor your insurance based on the activities you plan to undertake.

Loss or theft of personal belongings is another concern to address in your travel insurance policy. While Thailand is generally a safe destination, petty theft can happen in bustling marketplaces or crowded tourist spots. Having insurance that covers the loss of valuables like cameras, smartphones, and passports can save you from the significant expenses and inconveniences of replacing them abroad.

Beyond these practical aspects, choosing a travel insurance policy that offers 24/7 support in your language is invaluable. When I lost my luggage during a connecting flight to Bangkok, being able to communicate with an English-speaking agent made resolving my issue much faster and less daunting.

In essence, selecting the right travel insurance is about ensuring peace of mind. It lets you fully immerse yourself in the joys of exploring Thailand—from wandering through the ancient ruins of Ayutthaya to celebrating the vibrant Songkran festival, or simply enjoying the serene beaches of Krabi. With a good insurance plan, you're not just protecting your trip investment but also ensuring that your experiences remain joyous and your memories fond, without the shadows of "what if" looming over your adventure.

In conclusion, taking the time to carefully choose travel insurance tailored to the nature of your trip to Thailand is not just a necessity but a crucial step in crafting a truly carefree and memorable travel experience.

CHAPTER 4

NAVIGATION AND TRANSPORTATION

Navigating through Thailand is an adventure in itself, and understanding the myriad transportation options available can turn any trip from good to great. During my travels across this vibrant country, I've navigated city streets and rural paths, learning the nuances of each mode of transport, from the iconic tuk-tuk to the efficient rail service.

In this chapter, we'll dive into the variety of transportation choices you'll have in Thailand. The tuk-tuk, an experience not to be missed, offers a thrilling ride through the bustling streets, particularly in Bangkok where the energy of the city pulses day and night. But there's more to getting around than just hopping into one of these three-wheeled wonders. Thailand's rail services, including the Bangkok Skytrain (BTS) and the Metro (MRT), are a godsend for beating the often congested traffic and cover extensive parts of the metropolitan area, making them a great choice for tourists looking to explore the city efficiently.

For those who desire more independence, renting vehicles might be the way to go. Whether you choose a car, a motorbike, or even a bicycle, having your own wheels gives you the freedom to explore at your own pace. We'll explore how to rent these vehicles safely, what you need to know about local driving regulations, and tips for navigating Thailand's roads, which can range from well-paved highways to rural byways that offer scenic but challenging drives.

Additionally, we'll cover essential tips for using both public and private transportation in Thailand. From negotiating fares with local taxi drivers to understanding the etiquette of public transit, knowing these tips can enhance your travel experience, ensuring safety and convenience as you journey through the country.

Whether you're a first-timer in Thailand or a seasoned traveler, understanding how to navigate the transportation landscape here is crucial. This chapter aims to equip you with the knowledge to travel smart and enjoy the journey as much as the destination, ensuring every ride—be it on a slow train through the countryside or a speedy scooter down a coastal road—adds to your treasure trove of travel memories. With the right information, each trip can be safe, fun, and full of the expected and unexpected joys that traveling in Thailand brings.

Getting Around: Options from Tuk-Tuks to Rail Service
Navigating through Thailand offers an array of transport options, each with its unique flair and practicality. From my travels, the joy of exploring this vibrant country often lies in the journey as much as the destination, given the diverse

modes of transportation available, ranging from the traditional tuk-tuk to the modern rail services.

Tuk-Tuks—these iconic, three-wheeled vehicles are synonymous with Thailand and offer a fast, if not exhilarating, way to get around. Navigating through the streets in a tuk-tuk is an adventure itself, feeling the city's pulse with every turn and stop. Always agree on a fare before setting off, as these rides don't have meters. Riding a tuk-tuk at night, when the streets are aglow with neon lights and bustling night markets, transforms a simple commute into a vibrant tour of the city's lively nightlife.

Songthaews are another local option; these are pickup trucks adapted with rows of seats in the back. They function as shared taxis and are quite economical. I found them incredibly useful for shorter distances or when traveling within local neighborhoods. They're not only cheaper than private taxis but also provide a chance to interact with locals, sharing the ride and perhaps picking up recommendations for hidden gems in the area.

Motorbike taxis are a common sight, especially in congested areas where they maneuver through traffic much faster than four-wheeled vehicles. They're ideal for solo travelers looking to get somewhere quickly. Wearing a helmet is a must, not just for safety but because it's the law, and many motorbike taxi drivers provide an extra helmet for passengers.

Rail Service in Thailand includes the BTS Skytrain and MRT Metro, which are blessings for travelers in Bangkok. The Skytrain, with its extensive network, has been my lifeline on many occasions, whisking me above the city's traffic to major shopping, entertainment, and business districts. The MRT, although not as extensive, connects several key areas of Bangkok that are not accessible by the BTS, including the cultural heartland of old Bangkok. The rail systems are clean, efficient, and well-connected, with clear announcements and signs in both Thai and English, making them incredibly tourist-friendly.

For longer distances, Thailand's train system connects major cities with rural towns. My journey from Bangkok to Chiang Mai by train was a scenic delight, offering views of the countryside that are missed when flying. Trains in Thailand range from rapid services with air-conditioned cars to slower, local services where open windows invite breezy exchanges with the outside scenery.

Each of these transportation options provides its own experience and insight into Thai life. The tuk-tuk rides brought me closer to the vibrant chaos of Thailand's streets, the songthaews showed me the local's way of travel, and the rail services offered a respite from the heat and a chance to see the city from above. Choosing how to get around in Thailand isn't just about convenience; it's about choosing the experiences you want to have, each ride adding a layer to your travel stories in this beautiful country.

Renting Vehicles: Cars, Motorbikes, and Bicycles

Renting vehicles in Thailand offers a thrilling way to take control of your travel itinerary, providing the flexibility to explore at your own pace. Whether it's navigating the winding mountain roads in a car, zipping through bustling city streets on a motorbike, or leisurely biking along tranquil rural paths, the experiences are as varied as the landscapes.

Renting a Car: For those looking to cover longer distances or travel in groups, renting a car is ideal. The roads in much of Thailand, especially major cities and tourist spots, are well-maintained and signposted in both Thai and English, making navigation straightforward. My own experience renting a car to explore the northern reaches of Chiang Rai was liberating. It allowed me to stop at small hill tribe villages and hidden waterfalls, places that public transport simply doesn't reach. Always ensure you have a valid international driver's license and proper insurance, which are necessities for renting a car and driving in Thailand.

Motorbikes: Renting a motorbike is a popular choice among solo travelers and adventurers alike, providing an authentic and exhilarating way to embrace Thailand's vibrant street life and stunning natural beauty. From my adventures on Phuket's coastlines to the rural explorations in Pai, a motorbike brought an element of excitement and ease that other transport forms could not match. However, safety is paramount—always wear a helmet, drive defensively, and make sure you are comfortable with the bike before heading out. Most rental shops will offer you a brief test ride, and it's wise to take it to ensure everything works well.

Bicycles: For the environmentally conscious and fitness enthusiasts, bicycles are a fantastic option. Many tourist-friendly areas such as Sukhothai's historical parks and Bangkok's green belts have dedicated bike lanes and routes. Renting a bicycle can provide a serene and intimate way to connect with the local environment and culture. Riding through the ancient city of Ayutthaya, exploring its vast temple ruins at my own pace, was a highlight of my trip—peaceful, enriching, and quite a workout!

Tips for Renting: When renting any vehicle, it's crucial to check the condition before you start your journey. Look for signs of wear and tear, check the brakes, lights, and if applicable, the clutch. Always ask about the rental agency's emergency procedures and keep their contact information handy. Negotiating the rental rate and clarifying terms for fuel, mileage, and return conditions can also save you from unexpected charges.

Making the Experience Memorable: What truly makes renting vehicles in Thailand memorable is the sheer independence it grants you. Whether it's stopping by a roadside stall for fresh mango sticky rice, discovering a secluded beach, or joining in a local festival, having your own transport lets you dive deeper into Thailand's rich tapestry of experiences.

By choosing the mode of transport that best fits your travel style and needs, you can transform any trip into a deeply personal journey through one of the world's most diverse and scenic destinations. Renting a vehicle in Thailand isn't just about mobility; it's about crafting unforgettable moments that start the minute you turn the key.

Tips for Using Public and Private Transportation Safely

Navigating the bustling routes of Thailand's public and private transportation systems can be both an exhilarating and an eye-opening experience. From the first time I stepped onto a colorful, slightly rickety bus in downtown Bangkok to catching a late-night tuk-tuk back to my hotel, each ride has taught me something new about the rhythms of Thai life and how to travel safely.

Using Public Transportation

Thailand's public transportation network is extensive, especially in larger cities like Bangkok. The BTS Skytrain and MRT Metro are paragons of public transport efficiency, not only speeding you above or below the city's chronic traffic but also connecting you to major tourist destinations safely and economically. Always have a map handy—either on your phone or a physical copy. It helps to study routes before heading out, ensuring you know your stops and transfer points. Also, keep small bills and coins for tickets; while reloadable cards are available, cash is king for single journeys.

Safety on public transport is paramount. The Thai people are generally helpful and polite, but as in any bustling metropolis, keeping a watchful eye on your belongings is advisable. During my trips, I always kept my bag in front of me and avoided using my phone near train doors. These small precautions can prevent opportunistic theft.

Private Transportation: For more direct travel, tuk-tuks and taxis are readily available. Tuk-tuks are a must-try for any visitor—there's nothing quite like zipping through a Thai night, the city lights blurring past. However, it's essential to negotiate and agree on the fare before starting your journey. Some tuk-tuk drivers offer scenic routes at higher prices, which can be wonderful if you're not in a hurry and wish to see more of the city.

Taxis are metered, and it's wise to insist on using the meter to avoid overpaying. From experience, a polite but firm "Meter, please" at the start of your ride usually does the trick. For late-night travels, I found apps like Grab to be invaluable, providing safe, metered, and trackable rides without the hassle of negotiating.

Renting Vehicles: For those venturing outside urban areas, renting motorbikes or cars is popular. If you choose to rent a motorbike, ensure you are comfortable with the local driving style, which can be chaotic. Always wear a helmet, check the vehicle's condition, and ensure you have adequate insurance coverage.

In quieter areas, renting bicycles can offer a delightful way to explore. It's leisurely, eco-friendly, and gives you the flexibility to stop wherever and whenever you want, from roadside cafes to hidden temples off the beaten path.

General Safety Tips: Whether on public or private transport, always keep a local emergency number saved on your phone and have the address of your accommodation written in Thai—it can be a lifesaver in unexpected situations. Also, learning a few phrases in Thai to communicate with drivers and locals can enhance your experience significantly.

Exploring Thailand through its diverse transportation options allows you to experience the country's dynamic pace and scenic beauty firsthand. Each journey is more than just a route from point A to B; it's a chapter in your travel story, filled with vibrant imagery and interactions that paint a full picture of life in Thailand. As long as you travel with mindfulness and respect for the local customs and safety practices, you're set for an unforgettable adventure.

CHAPTER 5

ACCOMMODATION GUIDE

Finding the perfect place to stay in Thailand—a country where the warmth of its people is as famous as its sun-drenched beaches—can significantly enhance your travel experience. Throughout my travels here, I've learned that whether you settle into a cozy beachside villa, a lively hostel in the heart of Bangkok, or a luxurious resort hidden away in the mountains of Chiang Mai, each choice opens a different window into the vibrant life and culture of Thailand.

In this chapter, we'll delve into the array of accommodation options available across this beautiful land. From bustling hotels located in the urban centers to serene hostels that cater to budget-savvy backpackers and cultural explorers, understanding what each type offers is key to making an informed decision that suits your travel style and needs.

We will also explore some of the more unique lodging options such as homestays, where you can live with local families, sharing meals and stories, experiencing Thai hospitality firsthand. For those seeking solitude or a luxurious getaway, private villas and eco-resorts offer exclusive experiences that are both environmentally sustainable and indulgently relaxing.

Navigating through the reservation process can be fraught with pitfalls, from hidden fees to non-refundable policies. I'll share strategies to help you avoid these common traps, ensuring that you secure not just any accommodation, but the right one for you—places where you can rest, recharge, and perhaps even find a home away from home.

Each type of accommodation in Thailand offers its own set of benefits and experiences, and choosing wisely can turn a good vacation into an unforgettable one. Whether you're here to explore the bustling street markets, the serene temples, or the stunning natural landscapes, where you choose to lay your head at night is an integral part of your adventure. So, let's take a closer look at what each type of stay has to offer and how to secure the best spots that will make your Thai journey truly memorable.

Hotels, Hostels, and Resorts: Finding the Best Fit

Choosing the right accommodation in Thailand—whether it's a hotel, hostel, or resort—can dramatically enhance your travel experience, serving as your retreat after a day of adventures or your sanctuary to relax and rejuvenate.

Hotels in Thailand cater to a broad spectrum of travelers. For those who prioritize convenience and comfort, city hotels are often located near major attractions and transport hubs, making them an ideal base for exploring. These hotels range from budget-friendly options to luxury accommodations, and many offer amenities like swimming pools, in-house restaurants, and fitness centers. For example, staying at a well-located hotel in Bangkok allowed me to effortlessly visit nearby street markets and historical sites, retreat to my room to cool down, and then head out again—all without losing time.

Hostels are perfect for travelers looking to stretch their budgets and meet fellow travelers. Hostels in Thailand are some of the best in the world, offering clean facilities, social events, and sometimes even private rooms in addition to traditional dormitories. They are fantastic places to exchange travel stories and tips with international and local travelers alike. I fondly recall evenings spent in the common areas of a Chiang Mai hostel, plotting day trips with new friends, which enriched my experience and even changed my travel plans for the better.

Resorts in Thailand are a realm of their own, especially in coastal regions like Phuket or the islands of Koh Samui and Koh Phi Phi. These resorts often offer all-inclusive experiences that can include spa services, excursions, and dining. The serenity of staying in a beachfront resort, waking up to the sound of the ocean, and stepping straight onto the sand is something magical. Resorts cater to those seeking a more secluded, luxury experience, often featuring private beaches, personal service, and a focus on relaxation and wellness.

Choosing between these depends largely on your personal travel style, budget, and the kind of experience you want to have in Thailand. Are you here to explore extensively, or to unwind? Do you want the local immersion a hostel can provide, or the pampering that comes with a luxury resort? These are considerations to weigh up as you plan your stay.

No matter which type of accommodation you choose, each can significantly impact your stay, turning a simple trip into a collection of memorable experiences that resonate long after you return home. Each night's stay should offer not just a place to rest, but a place that complements your adventure—be it through luxury, location, or the chance to meet like-minded travelers.

Unique Lodging: Homestays, Villas, and Eco-Resorts
Exploring unique lodging options in Thailand offers a delightful alternative to conventional hotels and resorts, immersing you deeply in the local environment and culture. From the charm of homestays and luxury of private villas to the sustainable embrace of eco-resorts, Thailand provides a myriad of choices that cater to every traveler seeking a memorable experience.

Homestays provide a window into the Thai way of life like no other accommodation can. Staying with a local family, I found myself learning to cook traditional Thai dishes, participating in daily routines, and enjoying the warmth and hospitality that Thais are known for. Homestays are often located in rural areas or small towns, offering a peaceful retreat from the bustling tourist spots. This kind of accommodation is perfect for those who are eager to connect on a personal level with locals and gain insights into the subtleties of Thai culture.

Villas in Thailand are synonymous with luxury and exclusivity, offering a private escape with all the comforts of a high-end resort. Often located in breathtaking settings like the beachfronts of Koh Samui or the lush countryside of Chiang Mai, villas provide a serene haven where you can relax in a space entirely your own. Many villas come with private pools, personal chefs, and in-house spa treatments, making them ideal for families, couples, or groups looking to indulge in a lavish, tailored holiday experience.

Eco-Resorts are for those who prioritize sustainability without compromising on comfort. Thailand's eco-resorts allow you to enjoy the natural beauty of the country in structures built from natural materials, utilizing renewable energy and offering organic dining options. My stay at an eco-resort in the mountains of Northern Thailand was enlightening—it not only offered a tranquil retreat but also actively contributed to conservation efforts and supported local communities.

Each of these lodging options enhances your travel experience by providing more than just a place to sleep— they offer a chance to learn, relax, and connect in ways that standard hotels often cannot match. Whether it's waking up to the sounds of the jungle, enjoying a homemade breakfast with your host family, or watching the sunset from your private beachfront villa, the memories forged at these places stay with you long after your visit.

By choosing a homestay, villa, or eco-resort, you're not just booking accommodation, you're crafting an experience that echoes the diversity and richness of Thailand itself. Each stay becomes a chapter of your travel story, filled with its own unique flavors and moments, and a personal connection to the people and the land that make Thailand truly special.

Reservation Strategies: Avoiding Pitfalls

Navigating the reservation process for accommodations in Thailand can be as much an art as a science, especially when you're aiming to snag the perfect spot for your stay. Having traveled through Thailand multiple times, I've learned some key strategies to avoid common pitfalls that can turn an exciting holiday plan into a headache.

Early Reservations: One of the first lessons I learned was the benefit of booking early. Thailand's popularity as a tourist destination means that the best places can fill up quickly, especially during peak seasons like the cool months from November to February, and during major festivals. Early booking not only secures your spot but often secures better rates. For luxury accommodations or unique lodgings like boutique hotels, eco-resorts, or villas, this is particularly crucial as they tend to have limited availability and don't handle last-minute bookings as flexibly.

Reading Reviews: Before I book, I dive deep into recent reviews from other travelers. Sites like TripAdvisor or Booking.com can provide invaluable insights into what to expect in terms of service, cleanliness, and hidden charges. I remember one hotel in Phuket that looked fantastic online but had consistent recent reviews about its lack of upkeep. Reviews are a goldmine of information and can help you avoid places that might look good on paper (or screen) but don't live up to expectations in reality.

Understanding Cancellation Policies: Always check the cancellation policy before booking. This can vary significantly between establishments and even between different rates at the same hotel. I always opt for bookings that offer free cancellation up to a few days before the stay.

This flexibility is a safeguard against unexpected changes in travel plans and can save you from losing money if things don't go as planned.

Confirming Your Booking: Once booked, confirming directly with the hotel can prevent another common pitfall— arriving to find no record of your reservation. A quick email or phone call can ensure that everything is set, and it also gives you a chance to request any specific needs or preferences, like a quiet room or a late check-out.

Securing Proof: Always have a printed or digital copy of your booking confirmation and receipts when you travel. This proof is essential if there are any discrepancies at check-in, and it's also helpful for visa applications, as some countries may require proof of accommodations upon entry.

Navigating Local Booking Sites: Sometimes local booking platforms offer better deals or more comprehensive options, especially for local brands or smaller properties that may not be listed on international sites. Tools like Agoda are very popular in Thailand and can provide competitive rates and a wider selection of accommodations.

By employing these strategies, I've not only avoided many common travel pitfalls but also enjoyed a variety of accommodations that enhanced my experiences in Thailand—from the bustling streets of Bangkok to the serene beaches of Koh Tao. These tips aren't just about securing a place to sleep; they're about crafting your ideal travel experience, ensuring that where you stay is as memorable as what you explore.

CHAPTER 6

CULINARY DELIGHTS

Embarking on a culinary journey through Thailand is like stepping into a vibrant tapestry of flavors, colors, and aromas that seduce the senses at every turn. My own explorations of Thai cuisine have revealed not just the diversity of dishes, but also the depth of culture woven into each recipe passed down through generations. In this chapter, we will delve into an array of culinary experiences that Thailand has to offer, from the bustling street food stalls to exquisite gourmet tours, and even into the kitchens where these delightful dishes are born.

First, we'll discover the must-try dishes and where to find them. Thailand's culinary landscape is a treasure trove of gastronomic delights. Whether it's the spicy, herbaceous notes of a proper Thai green curry or the tangy zest of a fresh papaya salad, each dish tells a story. I remember my first taste of authentic Pad Thai wrapped in a delicate egg omelet; it was nothing like what I had tasted outside of Thailand— so robust and filled with texture.

Then, we will take to the streets on food safaris and gourmet tours that uncover hidden gems and local favorites. There's something profoundly joyful about wandering through a Thai night market, the air filled with sizzling sounds and sweet, spicy aromas, selecting skewers of grilled meats and freshly made spring rolls from vendors whose families have sold these specialties for decades.

For those with specific dietary preferences, fear not. Thailand's culinary world also embraces vegetarian and special diet options, with dishes that are as full-flavored as any traditional meal. Vegetarian versions of Pad Thai, vibrant curries made with tofu, and a myriad of tropical fruits and vegetables ensure that no one misses out on the feast.

Lastly, for those looking to bring a piece of Thai culinary magic home, joining a cooking class is a must. These schools offer a hands-on approach to learning traditional cooking methods, from selecting the perfect ingredients at local markets to the art of balancing those quintessential Thai flavors of sweet, sour, salty, and spicy.

Each meal in Thailand is more than just nourishment; it's an experience, a celebration of the rich, jubilant spirit of Thai culture. So, let's whet our appetites and prepare to dive into the delicious, unforgettable world of Thai cuisine.

Must-Try Dishes and Where to Find Them

Exploring the culinary delights of Thailand is like embarking on an epicurean journey that tantalizes the taste buds with every bite. As someone who has traversed this vibrant country, I've encountered an array of dishes that are not just meals but stories served on a plate, each originating from the different corners of Thailand.

One must-try dish is Pad Thai, a stir-fried noodle dish that is synonymous with Thai cuisine worldwide. Yet, nothing compares to enjoying it right where it was born. The best Pad Thai I've ever tasted was at a bustling street stall in Bangkok's Chinatown. The noodles were perfectly chewy, tossed with a tamarind-based sauce, and mixed with eggs, tofu, and shrimp, topped off with a sprinkle of crushed peanuts. It's a dish that perfectly balances sweet, sour, and salty, and is a quintessential Thai experience.

Another iconic dish is Som Tam (green papaya salad), which hails from the Northeast but has won hearts across the country. In a small, unassuming market near Silom in Bangkok, I found an old lady who mixed shredded green papaya with chilies, lime juice, fish sauce, and tomatoes, pounding all the ingredients in a mortar with such passion. Each bite was an explosion of spicy, sour, and sweetness—truly electrifying.

For those venturing to the north, Khao Soi is a must. This creamy coconut curry noodle soup is a specialty in Chiang Mai. Found at a popular local eatery just a short walk from the Tha Phae Gate, this dish served with chicken or beef, and topped with crispy noodles, shallots, and pickled mustard greens offers a rich texture and complexity of flavors that epitomize Northern Thai cuisine.

No culinary tour of Thailand would be complete without indulging in Massaman Curry, which I enjoyed in a small, family-run restaurant in the old city of Sukhothai. This rich curry with Persian roots is made with coconut milk, potatoes, onions, and meat—usually chicken or beef. It's a milder curry but deep in flavor with a subtle sweetness, perfect for those who prefer less spicy dishes.

Traveling south, Seafood is the star of the culinary show. In the coastal town of Hua Hin, seafood restaurants line the beach, offering freshly caught fish, crabs, and prawns grilled to perfection. Dining here as the sun sets over the Gulf of Thailand is as much about the atmosphere as it is about the fresh, salty flavors of the sea.

Each of these dishes represents a cornerstone of Thai cuisine and is best experienced in their locales, where the freshness of the ingredients and the authenticity of the preparation elevate the dining experience. Getting to these places is part of the adventure—whether by tuk-tuk, taxi, or a scenic train ride, each journey contributes to the rich tapestry of Thai culinary exploration.

Sampling these dishes not only satisfies the palate but also offers insights into the Thai way of life, where food is celebrated with enthusiasm and gratitude. It's a journey that goes beyond eating; it's about connecting with the people, understanding the culture, and making memories that linger long after the flavors fade.

Street Food Safaris and Gourmet Tours

Embarking on a street food safari in Thailand is an exhilarating experience that tantalizes the senses at every turn. Walking through the bustling streets and night markets, each stall offers a glimpse into the rich culinary traditions that Thailand proudly upholds. From sizzling woks in Bangkok to aromatic soups in Chiang Mai, the adventure is as much about discovering new flavors as it is about understanding the Thai culture.

One of the best places to start is Bangkok's famed Yaowarat Road in Chinatown, where the street comes alive at night with endless food stalls. Here, you can dive into dishes like Guay Jub, a peppery rolled noodle soup with crispy pork, or the sweet and tart Mango Sticky Rice. To reach Yaowarat, take the MRT to Hua Lamphong Station; from there, Chinatown is a short taxi or tuk-tuk ride away. Navigating these narrow alleys filled with golden ducks hanging in windows and steam rising from pots is a sensory overload that's quintessentially Bangkok.

In Chiang Mai, the Sunday Walking Street Market on Ratchadamnoen Road is a culinary delight waiting to be explored. This market is accessible by foot from the old city center, or by songthaew, a shared taxi-like vehicle that is extremely affordable. The streets here burst with flavors offering everything from Sai Oua, a spicy and herbaceous Northern Thai sausage, to Khao Soi, a creamy, curried noodle soup that has become synonymous with this city's cuisine.

For a more curated experience, gourmet food tours are available in most major tourist cities. These tours often start from designated meeting points easily accessible by public transport or provided shuttles. In Bangkok, for example, gourmet tours might begin in areas like Saphan Taksin, conveniently reached by the BTS Skytrain, which connects to shuttle boats that tour the historic Chao Phraya River. These tours don't just feed you; they educate you about the ingredients, history, and techniques behind famous dishes, often leading you into hidden alleys and to the tables of renowned street food chefs.

Beyond mere eating, these street food safaris and gourmet tours invite you to participate in the local way of life. They provide a platform to interact with locals, each vendor ready with a smile and often happy to share their culinary secrets with curious travelers. This interaction deepens the travel experience, making it more personal and memorable.

Whether you're sampling skewered meats grilled over open flames in Bangkok, savoring fresh papaya salad prepared before your eyes in a bustling market in Isaan, or enjoying a late-night snack under the neon lights of Pattaya, the street food of Thailand offers more than just sustenance. It offers a story, a taste of tradition passed down through generations, ready to be discovered by those eager enough to venture through the vibrant streets of this dynamic country.

Vegetarian and Special Diet Options

Navigating the culinary landscape of Thailand as a vegetarian or someone with specific dietary needs can initially seem like a daunting endeavor. However, during my travels through this beautiful country, I discovered that Thailand's food scene is incredibly accommodating and diverse, offering a wealth of options that cater to vegetarian, vegan, and gluten-free diets.

Thailand's cuisine is naturally rich in vegetables, fruits, and rice, making it inherently friendly to various dietary preferences. Tofu, a staple protein source in many Asian cuisines, is widely used across Thailand and is a fantastic substitute in dishes that typically contain meat. I found that most street food vendors and restaurants were very accommodating when I requested vegetarian options. The key is to learn a few phrases in Thai, such as "_Mangsawirat_" (vegetarian) or "_Kin jay_" (vegan), to communicate your dietary restrictions clearly.

One of the must-try dishes for vegetarians visiting Thailand is Pad Thai. This classic dish is usually made with shrimp or chicken, but you can easily find vegetarian versions made with tofu and without fish sauce. The best Pad Thai I enjoyed was at a small eatery in Bangkok's Banglamphu area, where the chef substituted soy sauce for fish sauce and added an extra serving of vegetables for a hearty meal.

Another delightful experience is exploring the local markets where vendors sell a dazzling array of fresh fruits like mangosteen, dragon fruit, and rambutan. These markets are not only a feast for the palate but also a visual spectacle. The Or Tor Kor Market in Bangkok, easily accessible by the MRT to Kamphaeng Phet station, is renowned for its fresh produce and has numerous stalls offering ready-to-eat vegetarian dishes, freshly squeezed juices, and vegan snacks.

For those seeking a deeper dive into Thai cuisine, Thailand boasts a range of vegetarian and vegan restaurants, especially in tourist hotspots like Chiang Mai and Phuket. Chiang Mai, in particular, is a haven for vegetarian dining, with cafes and restaurants like Anchan Vegetarian Restaurant where the menu changes weekly depending on the availability of local, seasonal ingredients.

Additionally, Thailand's Buddhist culture influences its cuisine, and during the annual Vegetarian Festival, particularly observed in Phuket, you'll find the country comes alive with vegetarian fare. This festival is a great time for food enthusiasts to experience an even wider variety of Thai vegetarian dishes.

Lastly, for those with a penchant for cooking, Thailand offers numerous cooking classes that cater to vegetarians and vegans. These classes not only teach you how to prepare traditional Thai dishes using plant-based ingredients but also often include a market tour to learn about local produce and spices.

Whether you're dining in the quaint cafes of Bangkok, the bustling markets of Chiang Mai, or the beachfront restaurants of Krabi, Thailand's culinary scene is wonderfully inclusive. With a little preparation and some basic Thai phrases, vegetarians and those on special diets will find Thailand a joy to explore, full of flavors that cater to every palate.

Culinary Journeys and Cooking Schools

One of the most enriching ways to dive deep into Thailand's culinary heart is by engaging directly in its food culture through culinary journeys and cooking schools. These experiences offer more than just meals; they provide a hands-on introduction to the Thai way of life, where food is both an art and a communal activity.

During my travels, I had the pleasure of participating in several cooking classes, which are offered prolifically throughout the country, from the mist-shrouded hills of the north to the sun-drenched islands of the south. These classes often begin with a visit to a local market. Accompanied by a chef, you get to explore rows of fresh produce, aromatic spices, and unique ingredients that are the building blocks of

Thai cuisine. This market visit is not only an eye-opener to the variety and freshness of Thai produce but also an excellent primer on how locals shop for and select their ingredients.

In Chiang Mai, a city renowned for its rich cultural heritage and artisanal food practices, I attended a cooking class that taught me how to make Khao Soi. This creamy, curried noodle soup is a northern Thai specialty, and learning to cook it within the rustic settings of an old Thai farmhouse was as delightful as it sounds. The class included grinding our own curry pastes, which is the secret to the dish's robust flavor.

Bangkok, Thailand's bustling capital, offers its own array of cooking schools where you can learn everything from street food favorites to royal Thai dishes. I found these classes to be highly interactive and personalized, often capped at a small number of participants to ensure everyone could actively participate. After preparing a range of dishes, like Pad Thai, Green Curry, and Mango Sticky Rice, we would sit down to enjoy our creations, accompanied by a well-deserved sense of accomplishment.

For those looking for something a bit more specialized, there are also culinary tours that focus on specific aspects of Thai cuisine, such as vegetarian cooking, seafood preparations, or the art of Thai desserts. These tours not only teach cooking techniques but also delve into the history and evolution of

Thai culinary traditions, making them a comprehensive cultural education.

These cooking schools and culinary tours are easily accessible. In larger cities like Bangkok and Chiang Mai, many schools offer pickup services from your accommodation. In more remote areas, you might need to arrange a taxi or tuk-tuk, but the destination is well worth the journey.

Participating in a Thai cooking class or culinary tour doesn't just enhance your cooking skills; it gives you stories to bring back home. Each dish comes with its own narrative, each technique a connection to a tradition several centuries old, allowing you to bring a piece of Thailand into your kitchen. This immersive approach turns each meal into a celebration of Thai heritage, making it an unforgettable part of your travel experience.

CHAPTER 7

SHOPPING AND LEISURE

Exploring the vibrant shopping scene in Thailand is an essential part of the travel experience here, offering everything from glittering malls to bustling markets where the air buzzes with the excitement of discovery and negotiation. During my journeys, I've found that shopping in Thailand isn't just about acquiring things; it's an adventure into the heart of Thai culture.

In this chapter, we dive into the expansive world of Shopping in Thailand: Malls to Markets. Thailand's malls are air-conditioned oases that offer a respite from the tropical heat and a glimpse into the country's modern consumer culture. Places like the iconic MBK Center or the luxurious Siam Paragon in Bangkok provide a dizzying array of goods, from high-end designer labels to affordable fashion and electronics. Contrastingly, the markets such as Chatuchak Weekend Market or the night markets in Chiang Mai, with their labyrinthine alleys teeming with artisan crafts, street food, and clothing, offer a more traditional shopping experience where senses are treated to a carnival of sights, sounds, and smells.

Next, we'll explore the Souvenir Guide: Authentic Crafts and Gifts. Thailand is renowned for its craftsmanship in goods such as silk, ceramics, teak products, and intricate silver jewelry. I remember the joy of selecting a hand-painted ceramic bowl in Lampang — a region famous for its pottery — and learning about the skill and history behind each piece. This section will help you identify and choose meaningful souvenirs that are not only a memento of your travels but also support the artisan communities.

We'll also provide essential Bargaining Tips: Do's and Don'ts. Bargaining is an integral part of the shopping experience in many Thai markets. Knowing how to do it respectfully and effectively can enhance your shopping experience significantly. For instance, a friendly smile and a polite request for a "special price" can often lead to a more favorable bargain. However, it's also important to know when to stop bargaining, as understanding and respecting the seller's minimum price preserves dignity on both sides.

From the air-conditioned, gleaming malls to the vibrant stalls of the local markets, shopping in Thailand is a dynamic blend of old and new. This chapter will not only prepare you to navigate these shopping venues with confidence but also help you enjoy them as a local would, with all the insider knowledge and none of the tourist faux pas. Whether you're looking for luxury goods or traditional crafts, the stories you collect from these shopping excursions will add another layer of rich texture to your Thai adventure.

Shopping in Thailand: Malls to Markets

Exploring the shopping landscape in Thailand is a journey as dynamic and varied as the country itself, blending high-end luxury with traditional markets that buzz with the vibrant day-to-day life of the Thai people. From the sleek, air-conditioned malls of Bangkok to the sprawling, bustling markets found in almost every town, shopping in Thailand caters to every taste and budget.

In Bangkok, the shopping experience is as grand as it is diverse. The Siam Paragon, located right at Siam BTS Skytrain station, is a cornerstone of luxury shopping in the city. This mammoth mall houses everything from high-end fashion brands like Louis Vuitton and Prada to Southeast Asia's largest aquarium, an expansive gourmet market, and a multiplex cinema. Just a stone's throw away is MBK Center, a contrasting scene where both tourists and locals haggle over a wide range of merchandise, from cheap clothes and mobile phones to souvenir trinkets. Navigating through these malls offers more than just retail therapy; it's a cool escape from the city's humid embrace and a peek into Thailand's modern consumer culture.

Venturing out from Bangkok, the shopping experience shifts dramatically as you explore the local markets, each brimming with character and history. Chatuchak Weekend Market, accessible via Mo Chit BTS station or Chatuchak Park MRT station, is a must-visit. This sprawling market with over 8,000 stalls offers a little bit of everything, from vintage clothing and antiques to live animals and delicious street food. The thrill of the hunt and the joy of unearthing treasures here make it a paradise for bargain hunters.

In Chiang Mai, the Sunday Walking Street Market stretches along Ratchadamnoen Road in the old city from Tha Pae Gate. This market transforms the street into a lively festival of crafts, art, music, and food every Sunday evening. Here, the focus is on hand-made local crafts and street food, offering a taste of Northern Thai culture. You can reach the start of this market by songthaew or tuk-tuk, which are readily available throughout the city.

For those interested in more authentic and traditional Thai shopping experiences, the floating markets around Bangkok offer a unique vibe. Damnoen Saduak, while quite touristy, still presents colorful boatloads of vendors selling tropical fruits, vegetables, and local foods directly from their boats. Located about an hour and a half from Bangkok, it's most easily reached by joining a guided tour, which often includes round-trip transportation.

Shopping in Thailand is also about embracing the local way of life; it's about pausing to sip Thai iced tea from a street vendor as you juggle shopping bags, or the moment of shared laughter with a local artisan as you attempt to speak a few words of Thai. Each market stall, shopping street, and gleaming mall tells a story, offering insights into the kingdom's rich tapestry of history, culture, and modernity.

Whether you're searching for the perfect souvenir, the latest fashion, or exotic Thai spices, the markets and malls of Thailand provide a shopping experience that is as fulfilling as it is unforgettable.

Souvenir Guide: Authentic Crafts and Gifts

One of the joys of traveling through Thailand is discovering the rich tapestry of its local crafts and souvenirs. Each region offers something unique, reflecting the local culture, traditions, and skills passed down through generations. Whether you're wandering through the bustling markets of Bangkok or exploring the artisan villages in the northern provinces, the search for authentic Thai crafts and gifts can be as rewarding as the treasures you take home.

During my travels, I've been captivated by the variety and quality of Thai handicrafts, which make perfect mementos and gifts. One must-purchase item is Thai silk, known worldwide for its quality and beauty. In Bangkok, I visited Jim Thompson's House, where you can not only buy beautifully crafted silk products but also learn about the fascinating history of the silk industry in Thailand. The vibrant colors and intricate patterns make each piece of fabric or clothing truly special.

Another iconic souvenir is teakwood carvings from Chiang Mai. The skillful craftsmanship is evident in the elaborate designs, which range from small trinkets to large furniture pieces. The Night Bazaar in Chiang Mai is an excellent place to find these, and you can watch artisans at work, chiseling out intricate patterns that tell stories of Thai mythology and daily life.

For those interested in pottery, the village of Koh Kret, just outside of Bangkok, offers an extraordinary insight into the craft of pottery-making. The Mon community here is known for their distinctive style of pottery, which is unglazed but beautifully engraved. Taking a day trip here not only allows you to pick up a unique piece directly from the artisans but also offers a peek into the island's tranquil rural life.

No visit to Thailand is complete without bringing back some of the country's famed spices. Places like the Or Tor Kor Market in Bangkok provide a dazzling array of fresh spices that can transport the flavors of Thai cuisine to your kitchen. From fragrant lemongrass to fiery bird's eye chilies, packing some of these spices means you're taking home more than just objects—you're bringing back the taste of Thailand.

Lastly, for those who appreciate jewelry, the silverware from the Karen hill tribe in northern Thailand is a perfect pick. Each piece is handcrafted and distinct, often featuring designs inspired by nature and tribal culture. The Saturday Walking Street Market in Chiang Mai is a great spot to find these exquisite silver pieces.

Shopping for these items isn't just about the acquisition; it's about the experience. It's about the gentle haggle over price, the smiles and nods of a local craftsman as you admire their work, and the knowledge that with every purchase, you're helping to sustain traditional crafts. These souvenirs carry with them not just the beauty of Thai craft but also stories and memories of your travels. They are tangible pieces of a journey that continues to resonate long after you've returned home.

Bargaining Tips: Do's and Don'ts

Navigating the art of bargaining in Thailand is an integral part of the shopping experience, especially in markets and street stalls where the price often isn't set in stone. From my own experiences, mastering a few key bargaining techniques not only ensures you get a good deal but also adds a layer of interaction with the local culture that can be both fun and respectful.

Do: Start with a Smile and Friendly Greeting
Thais appreciate courtesy and a light-hearted approach. A smile goes a long way and starting the interaction with a friendly "Sawasdee khrap/kha" (hello) sets a positive tone. It shows respect, and you're more likely to get a friendly response.

Do: Learn to Say 'Too Expensive' in Thai
Saying "Pang mak" (too expensive) in a playful manner can break the ice and show that you know your stuff. It often leads to a chuckle and more reasonable counter offers. It's a simple phrase but shows that you're trying to engage with the language and culture.

Do: Know the Market Value
Before you start bargaining, it's crucial to have a rough idea of what items should cost. I usually spend some time browsing or asking prices at different stalls to get a sense of the going rates. This research helps in knowing when to push for a better price or when a deal is fair.

Don't: Offer Too Low
While it's common to bargain, offering a price that's too low can be seen as disrespectful. I learned to usually start at about 30% lower than the offered price and expect to meet

somewhere in the middle. It's a negotiation dance that both parties are in on.

Don't: Show Too Much Enthusiasm
If you find something you really like, try to contain your excitement. Vendors can tell when you've fallen in love with an item, and they might stick to a higher price knowing you're likely to pay it. Play it cool, and keep your poker face on.

Do: Walk Away if Necessary
Sometimes, walking away is part of the strategy. More often than not, if the seller can lower their price, they'll call you back. If they don't, either the price was fair or you can find a similar item elsewhere.

Don't: Bargain Just to Bargain
If the price is already reasonable and you're happy with it, especially for lower-cost items, it's sometimes better to just pay the asking price. Bargaining hard over every little thing can waste time and isn't always worth the savings.

Do: Be Prepared to Pay in Cash
Many market vendors don't take credit cards. Having cash not only makes transactions easier but also helps in bargaining, as it offers immediate payment. Keep smaller denominations handy because not all vendors have change for large bills.

Do: Enjoy the Process
Bargaining in Thailand shouldn't be a stressful ordeal—it's part of the shopping culture and is often done with a smile. Engaging in this way can be a joyful, culturally immersive experience. You'll learn more about the local way of life, make some human connections, and even have fun.

Each of these tips has helped me turn every bargaining opportunity into a memorable part of my travels in Thailand, filled with friendly banter, learning, and, of course, great finds.

CHAPTER 8

EXPLORING MAJOR REGIONS

Thailand is a country of staggering diversity, offering a tapestry of experiences that can transform any traveler's understanding of beauty, culture, and adventure. From the bustling streets of Bangkok to the serene heights of the northern mountains, each region boasts its own unique identity, stories, and attractions. As we delve into the major regions of Thailand, you'll discover the distinct flavors and sights that make this country a treasure trove for explorers.

Bangkok: The Heart of Thailand—the vibrant capital where traditional meets contemporary. The city pulses with life, offering everything from glittering temples and palaces to some of the world's most visited markets and malls. My own journeys through Bangkok have taught me that every corner of this metropolis has a new facet to explore, be it culinary delights by street vendors or the serene spaces within the Grand Palace.

The North: Chiang Mai, Chiang Rai, and the Golden Triangle—a region known for its mist-covered mountains and lush landscapes. Here, the air carries the scent of history and the coolness of the highlands. The cultural depth of Chiang Mai, with its hundreds of temples, contrasts sharply with the rugged adventures awaiting in Chiang Rai and the fabled Golden Triangle at the confluence of Thailand, Laos, and Myanmar.

The Northeast: Isan's Heritage and Natural Wonders—often overlooked by typical travel itineraries, Isan offers an unspoiled glimpse into Thailand's rural life. It's a region rich in archaeological marvels, like the ancient temples of Khmer heritage and national parks that are home to some of the country's most thrilling wildlife encounters.

The East: Pattaya, Koh Samet, and Rayong—areas that serve as perfect getaways with their stunning beaches and buzzing nightlife. Pattaya constantly reinvents itself as a destination for luxury and leisure, while Koh Samet and Rayong offer more laid-back beach experiences, ideal for those looking to escape the hustle and bustle.

The South: Phuket, Krabi, and the Gulf Islands—the ultimate beach destinations, where limestone cliffs and turquoise waters create postcard-perfect scenes. Phuket combines natural beauty with opulent tourist facilities, making it a top choice for travelers seeking both relaxation and entertainment, whereas Krabi offers tranquil beaches ideal for snorkeling and kayaking.

As we explore these regions, each with its own allure and character, you'll find that Thailand is not just a place to visit, but a world to experience. Each destination tells part of Thailand's grand narrative, inviting you to weave your own stories through the landscapes, cultures, and interactions you will encounter. Whether you're a first-time visitor or returning, the depth and breadth of what you can discover here are bound to captivate and inspire.

Bangkok: The Heart of Thailand

Bangkok, often referred to as the heart of Thailand, pulses with an energy that perfectly encapsulates the blend of traditional charm and modern dynamism that defines much of Southeast Asia. This sprawling metropolis, set on the banks of the Chao Phraya River, is where you can witness monks robed in saffron making their morning alms rounds just streets away from bustling markets and towering skyscrapers.

Navigating Bangkok is an adventure in itself. The city is accessible from almost anywhere in the world and serves as a major hub for international travel with two main airports: Suvarnabhumi Airport and Don Mueang International Airport. From either, the city center is reachable via taxi, bus, or the Airport Rail Link that connects to the Skytrain and underground systems, making it easy to dive straight into the heart of Bangkok upon arrival.

Accommodation options in Bangkok range from luxurious high-rise hotels to charming boutique accommodations that offer a glimpse into the city's local flavor. One such gem is The Siam Hotel, located a little away from the usual tourist hustle but right on the river, offering a serene escape with a view. Its proximity to the less crowded, more authentically local Thonburi side of Bangkok also makes it an excellent base for exploring the city in a more relaxed style.

For dining, Bangkok boasts an unrivaled street food scene that Michelin stars have even recognized. However, for a truly memorable dining experience, one might venture into the fine dining realm at establishments like Gaggan, repeatedly named the best restaurant in Asia, where Indian cuisine meets innovative molecular gastronomy. For those looking for something uniquely Thai, Nahm emphasizes traditional Thai dishes sourced from historical cookbooks, which is a culinary exploration of Thailand's heritage.

But Bangkok isn't just about luxurious stays and avant-garde cuisine; it's a city with layers. The Grand Palace and Wat Phra Kaew are quintessentially Bangkok, with their glittering facades and deep cultural significance. Meanwhile, areas like Siam and Sukhumvit buzz with shopping malls and nightlife. For a taste of local life, one might explore the labyrinthine alleys of Chinatown or the relaxed flow of the Chao Phraya River on a longtail boat.

Each visit to Bangkok offers a new perspective, a new flavor, and a new story. It's a city that beckons not just to be visited, but to be experienced—where every corner offers a new adventure, and every moment is an opportunity to create lasting memories. Whether you're here for the history, the food, the shopping, or simply to soak in the Thai culture, Bangkok delivers an exhilarating and enriching experience.

The North: Chiang Mai, Chiang Rai, and the Golden Triangle

Traveling through the northern region of Thailand, which includes Chiang Mai, Chiang Rai, and the Golden Triangle, feels like stepping into a different world—one marked by mist-shrouded mountains, ancient temples, and vibrant hill tribes. This part of Thailand holds a deep historical significance and a slower, more contemplative pace of life compared to the frenetic energy of Bangkok.

Chiang Mai, often considered the cultural capital of the north, is where traditional Thai culture intertwines seamlessly with modern life. Nestled among forested foothills, this city is more laid-back than Thailand's capital, yet no less vibrant. Chiang Mai is accessible by plane, with its international airport offering numerous daily flights from Bangkok and other major Asian cities. Alternatively, an overnight train from Bangkok to Chiang Mai can be a scenic, if slower, option.

In Chiang Mai, the Old City holds much of the charm, with its moat and crumbling walls speaking of a bygone era. The city is a haven for artisans, and visiting local markets like the Saturday Night Walking Street on Wualai Road allows you to appreciate the handmade textiles, pottery, and woodcarvings. For accommodations, the Dhara Dhevi Chiang Mai, designed like an ancient Lanna kingdom, offers a luxury stay unlike any other, with sprawling grounds and sublime spa treatments.

Chiang Rai, a three-hour drive northeast of Chiang Mai, serves as the gateway to the Golden Triangle. This city is known for its unique contemporary temples, like the striking White Temple (Wat Rong Khun), which blends traditional Buddhist temple architecture with surreal, modern elements. The Baan Dam Museum, or Black House, provides a fascinating contrast, featuring works by Thai artist Thawan Duchanee that explore darker themes.

The Golden Triangle, where the borders of Thailand, Laos, and Myanmar converge, is rich in history and natural beauty. The region was once notorious as one of the most prolific opium-producing areas in the world. Today, it's a destination for those interested in the area's history and indigenous cultures. A boat trip on the mighty Mekong River offers views of all three countries and an understanding of how interconnected they are. The Anantara Golden Triangle Elephant Camp & Resort in Chiang Rai provides an unforgettable experience where you can also participate in walking with elephants in a respectful and sustainable manner.

For dining in Chiang Mai, a meal at David's Kitchen offers a fine dining experience that combines French and Thai cuisines, perfect for an evening where you desire something a bit more refined. Alternatively, exploring local dishes like Khao Soi, a northern-style curry noodle soup, at a small eatery such as Khao Soi Khun Yai, gives you a taste of local flavors that are both rich and comforting.

Exploring Northern Thailand is like uncovering a hidden chapter of a history book. It's an experience that deepens your appreciation of Thailand's diversity, connecting you with its past and present in profound and lasting ways. Whether wandering through the ancient temple ruins, participating in traditional festivals, or simply enjoying the cool climate of the mountainous landscape, the north offers a distinctly different pace and perspective on Thai life that is not to be missed.

The Northeast: Isan's Heritage and Natural Wonders

The Northeast of Thailand, commonly known as Isan, is an area teeming with cultural heritage and natural wonders, often overlooked by the typical tourist itineraries that favor the country's southern beaches and northern mountains. However, Isan offers an authentic glimpse into a rural Thailand dotted with rice fields, forested temples, and vibrant local festivals.

Isan is bordered by the Mekong River to the north and east, which separates Thailand from Laos, and by Cambodia to the south. The region is easily accessible by plane, with several local airports like those in Udon Thani and Khon Kaen offering daily flights from Bangkok. Alternatively, many choose to travel by overnight train or bus, which, while slower, provides a scenic view of the Thai countryside transitioning into the distinct landscape of the Khorat Plateau.

One of the most striking features of Isan is its historical sites, particularly those related to the ancient Khmer Empire. The Phanom Rung Historical Park in Buriram is a stunning example, where a thousand-year-old Khmer temple sits atop an extinct volcano. This Hindu temple, dedicated to Shiva, is best visited during the annual Phanom Rung Festival when the sunrise aligns perfectly through the sanctum's doors, creating a breathtaking spectacle. Nearby, the village of Nang Rong serves as a convenient base for exploration, with guesthouses and local eateries that offer a warm, if rustic, welcome.

Khon Kaen, one of the major cities in Isan, presents an excellent blend of urban and rural Thai life. The city itself is a hub of silk production, with numerous shops selling hand-woven silk fabrics that Isan is famed for. The Khon Kaen National Museum provides an insightful look into the region's history, displaying artifacts from the prehistoric to the Dvaravati, Khmer, and Lan Xang eras. Dining in Khon Kaen offers the chance to try some of the region's unique dishes, such as som tam (spicy green papaya salad), which comes in many local variations that are spicier and more flavorful than those found in other parts of Thailand.

For those seeking natural beauty, the Ubon Ratchathani province offers the Pha Taem National Park, where you can find prehistoric cave paintings along cliffs overlooking the Mekong River. This area is less frequented by international tourists, providing a peaceful retreat into nature.

Accommodation options in Isan range from simple homestays and local guesthouses to more upscale resorts near major attractions. A particularly memorable place to stay is the Supanniga Home in Khon Kaen, which offers beautifully designed villas surrounded by gardens, combining modern amenities with traditional Thai architecture.

Exploring Isan is like peeling back layers of a deeply storied land that offers everything from archaeological treasures to natural escapes. Each visit brings deeper insight into the resilient and warm-hearted culture of Thailand's northeast, where the pace of life is slow, the landscapes are vast, and the smiles are unforgettable. For anyone looking to see beyond Thailand's typical tourist paths, Isan offers a journey back in time and a chance to connect with the heart and soul of rural Thai culture.

The East: Pattaya, Koh Samet, and Rayong

The eastern coast of Thailand, encompassing Pattaya, Koh Samet, and Rayong, offers a distinct blend of vibrant nightlife, serene beaches, and authentic cultural experiences that cater to all kinds of travelers. From bustling beach resorts to quiet islands, this region showcases a side of Thailand that balances tourist attractions with local life.

Pattaya is perhaps the most well-known destination in this part of Thailand, famous—or infamous—for its lively and often wild nightlife. Yet, beyond its party-centric reputation, Pattaya has evolved to include family-friendly attractions such as the Sanctuary of Truth, a stunning teak structure that represents the use of art as a reflection of the complexity of human philosophy. Pattaya is easily accessible, just a two-hour drive from Bangkok, making it a popular weekend getaway for locals and tourists alike. The city also offers a range of accommodations from luxury resorts like the Hilton Pattaya, known for its exquisite service and panoramic views of Pattaya Bay, to more budget-friendly options that still offer considerable comfort and convenience.

Traveling further from the hustle and bustle, Koh Samet offers a more laid-back vibe. This small island, part of the Khao Laem Ya–Mu Ko Samet National Park, is famous for its stunning white sand beaches, crystal clear waters, and the more relaxed atmosphere that is perhaps a bit harder to find in Pattaya. Koh Samet is just a short boat ride from Rayong's Ban Phe Pier, which itself is accessible by bus or car from

Bangkok in about three hours. Once on the island, the pace slows considerably: the roads are few, and beaches like Sai Kaew and Ao Prao are perfect for days spent sunbathing or enjoying water sports. For accommodation, Sai Kaew Beach Resort offers a comfortable stay with direct access to the beach and amenities that highlight the natural beauty of the island.

Rayong, the least touristy of the three, is the gateway to Koh Samet and a province known for its fruit plantations and seafood. Staying in Rayong offers a chance to explore local markets bustling with fresh produce and seafood, which reflects the region's agricultural and coastal heritage. One of the best places to enjoy fresh seafood is at Ban Phe, where restaurants line the waterfront, offering dishes like grilled prawns and spicy fish curry that are as fresh as they are flavorful.

For those interested in environmental conservation, Rayong is also home to the Sea Turtle Conservation Center, which focuses on the protection of sea turtles and their habitats. Visiting here provides a deeper understanding of Thailand's efforts in marine conservation.

Exploring this eastern trio gives travelers a well-rounded experience of Thailand's diverse offerings—from city nightlife to serene beaches and authentic local cuisine. Each destination serves up its unique set of adventures, making eastern Thailand a compelling region for those who wish to see beyond the typical tourist paths and delve deeper into the Thai way of life. Whether you're sunbathing on the tranquil beaches of Koh Samet, exploring the cultural sites in Pattaya, or enjoying the freshest seafood in Rayong, the east coast of Thailand holds treasures that promise to enrich your travel experience.

The South: Phuket, Krabi, and the Gulf Islands

Exploring the southern region of Thailand is like discovering a paradise that offers an idyllic blend of luxurious relaxation and adventurous activities. This part of Thailand, encompassing Phuket, Krabi, and the numerous Gulf Islands, is renowned for its crystal-clear waters, towering limestone cliffs, and vibrant nightlife, making it a premier destination for travelers from around the world.

Phuket, Thailand's largest island, is often the gateway for many visitors to the south. Accessible by air with its international airport serving flights from major global cities, or by road and sea from other parts of Thailand, Phuket is a hub of activity. From the bustling beaches of Patong, known for their vibrant nightlife, to the quieter shores of Kata and Karon, there is something for every type of traveler. For those seeking luxury accommodation, the Amanpuri resort offers an exclusive and serene experience with private villas, a secluded beach, and world-class service. Dining in Phuket is a delight, especially at restaurants like Baan Rim Pa, which offers Royal Thai cuisine with views over the Andaman Sea that are as spectacular as the food.

Moving east from Phuket, Krabi presents a more laid-back atmosphere but no less spectacular in terms of natural beauty. Krabi is accessible by road from Phuket and also has an airport serving domestic and international flights. This region is famous for its limestone cliffs and dense mangrove forests, and nowhere is this more beautifully showcased than at Railay Beach. Only accessible by boat, Railay offers stunning rock climbing opportunities that attract enthusiasts from around the globe. For accommodation, the Rayavadee Resort is nestled amidst the cliffs and beaches of the Railay Peninsula, providing luxury in harmony with nature. Dining in Krabi, I recommend the Grotto at Rayavadee, where you can eat beneath an ancient limestone cliff on the edge of the beach.

Lastly, the Gulf Islands such as Koh Samui, Koh Phangan, and Koh Tao, offer a slower pace still. Koh Samui is the most developed of these islands, with an international airport and a variety of experiences from bustling beach scenes at Chaweng Beach to the serene luxury of Bophut's Fisherman's Village. Koh Phangan is famous for its Full Moon Parties, but away from the party beaches, it offers quiet resorts perfect for relaxation. Koh Tao, while smaller, is one of the world's premier diving destinations, with affordable dive courses and vibrant coral reefs.

Whether staying in the ornate pavilions of The Four Seasons Resort Koh Samui, nestled among groves of coconut trees, or dining on the beach at The Dining on the Rocks restaurant, which offers innovative cuisine with panoramic views of the Gulf of Thailand, the southern region offers endless opportunities for memorable experiences.

The south of Thailand encapsulates the dream of a tropical paradise with its warm waters, stunning landscapes, and lush accommodations. It invites everyone to slow down and soak in the vibrant beauty, from the bustling markets and beach parties to the serene sunsets and luxurious quietude. Whether exploring the underwater marvels of Koh Tao, indulging in the nightlife of Phuket, or climbing the iconic cliffs of Krabi, southern Thailand remains a profoundly compelling destination that promises enchanting memories.

CHAPTER 9

LESSER-KNOWN GEMS

Thailand, a country known for its vibrant cities and stunning beaches, also harbors lesser-known gems that promise adventures beyond the typical tourist trails. In this chapter, we explore these hidden treasures, each offering a unique glimpse into Thailand's rich tapestry of culture, history, and natural beauty.

Our journey begins with the hidden towns and secret spots scattered across the country. These places are where Thailand's heart beats strongest, away from the bustling crowds and into the serene landscapes and untouched locales. From the quaint riverside communities in the north to the rugged, unexplored beaches of the south, each destination has its own story waiting to be discovered.

Ayutthaya, once the thriving capital of the Kingdom of Siam, now stands as a compelling archaeological site just a short train ride from Bangkok. The city's ancient ruins, some of which date back to the 14th century, tell tales of Thailand's former glory and grandeur. Wandering through these ruins, especially at sunset, one can't help but feel transported back in time, amidst the towering stupas and serene Buddha statues.

Moving northward, Sukhothai, Thailand's first capital, offers a quieter but equally profound historical experience. Its well-preserved ruins reflect the architectural and cultural zenith of early Thai civilization. Biking through the historical park, with its massive Buddha figures and intricate carvings, is like flipping through pages of a vivid history book, where each structure narrates a piece of Thailand's rich heritage.

Further from the mainland, the chapter explores Koh Samui and beyond. While Koh Samui is relatively well-known, the surrounding islands remain shrouded in mystery, offering secluded beaches, hidden coves, and untouched coral reefs. Venturing to places like Koh Tao or the less frequented Koh Phangan's northeastern coast reveals a side of island life that few tourists get to see—peaceful, untouched, and raw.

In writing this chapter, I invite you to look beyond the well-trodden paths and discover the lesser-known corners of Thailand. These places, rich with history, culture, and natural beauty, offer more than just a break from the crowded tourist spots; they provide a deeper understanding of Thailand's soul. Whether it's walking through the ruins of ancient cities, exploring the natural beauty of remote islands, or simply experiencing the everyday life of hidden towns, these gems enrich your travel experience with memories that are uniquely profound and personal.

Discovering Hidden Towns and Secret Spots

Discovering the hidden towns and secret spots of Thailand provides an opportunity to peel back the layers of popular tourist destinations to reveal the heart and soul of the country. These lesser-known locales offer an authentic glimpse into the everyday lives of the Thai people, away from the well-trodden paths frequented by tourists.

One such hidden gem is Phetchaburi, located just a couple of hours' drive from Bangkok. Despite its proximity to the capital, Phetchaburi feels worlds apart with its quiet streets lined with old shophouses and a slower pace of life. The historical park here is home to ancient temples and palaces like Phra Nakhon Khiri, which beautifully illustrates the blend of Thai and European architecture. Phetchaburi is accessible via a simple train ride from Bangkok, making it an easy but rewarding detour.

Further to the east, the small town of Trat offers a gateway to some of Thailand's most untouched islands, but it is also worth visiting in its own right. With its charming market, where locals shop for fresh seafood and traditional crafts, and its quaint, colonial-style buildings, Trat is a snapshot of local life. From here, ferries run to the lesser-known island of Koh Kood, where you can find some of Thailand's clearest waters and quietest beaches. Accommodation in Trat itself maintains a low profile, with guesthouses and small hotels such as the Artist's Place Trat offering cozy, budget-friendly rooms with a personal touch.

In the North, the town of Nan stands out for its rich heritage and serene landscape. Far from the usual tourist circuit, Nan features stunning temples like Wat Phumin, which houses some of the country's most exquisite murals depicting rural Thai life. The slow life here is punctuated by the gentle rhythms of the countryside and traditional teak wood houses. To reach Nan, one can take a direct flight from Bangkok or a more scenic route by bus or car through the northern highlands.

A perfect day in these towns often ends with dining at a local eatery that serves dishes not commonly found in the typical tourist areas. In Nan, for instance, the Night Food Market provides a culinary adventure where one can try northern delicacies such as *khao soi* and *sai oua* that are prepared with a distinct local flavor.

Each hidden town and secret spot in Thailand offers a unique narrative, one that is constructed less by the influx of tourists and more by the generations of families that have shaped its contours. Staying in these places, even just for a few days, allows one to see beyond the façade of Thailand's tourist industry and into the vibrant, beating heart of Thai culture. Whether you're wandering through the sleepy streets of Phetchaburi, exploring the untouched nature of Trat, or delving into the rich cultural tapestry of Nan, these destinations promise a more personal and profound understanding of Thailand.

Ayutthaya: A Journey Through Ancient Kingdoms

Exploring Ayutthaya, Thailand's ancient capital, is akin to stepping back in time to a kingdom that flourished from the 14th to the 18th centuries. Once a prosperous and cosmopolitan urban center and now a revered UNESCO World Heritage site, Ayutthaya presents a landscape filled with hauntingly beautiful temple ruins, statues of Buddha draped in saffron robes, and vast complexes that speak volumes of its former glory.

Located just about 80 kilometers north of Bangkok, Ayutthaya is easily accessible by road, rail, or river. Many visitors opt to take a scenic train journey from Bangkok's Hua Lamphong Station, which offers a slow yet intimate glimpse into the rural landscapes of central Thailand. Alternatively, traveling by road via bus or car can be quicker, and for those looking for a truly memorable experience, river cruises from Bangkok provide a serene passage along the Chao Phraya River leading directly into the heart of Ayutthaya.

Upon arriving, the historical park, which encompasses the ruins spread across the city, can be explored by bicycle, tuk-tuk, or even on foot. One of the first stops for many is Wat Phra Si Sanphet. Standing before its iconic row of chedis (stupas) that house the ashes of Ayutthayan kings, one can't help but feel the palpable pulse of history that courses through the site. Another not-to-miss spot is Wat Mahathat, where you can witness the surreal sight of a Buddha's head entwined within the roots of an overgrown banyan tree—an image that has become synonymous with Ayutthaya.

For those who delve deeper, the lesser-visited Wat Chaiwatthanaram on the riverbank offers sublime sunset views, with its lofty towers casting long shadows over the placid waters below. This temple complex offers a quieter moment to reflect on the rise and fall of this once magnificent city, sacked by the Burmese in the 18th century, leading to its abandonment.

Staying in Ayutthaya, visitors often choose accommodations that complement the historical experience. The classic Sala Ayutthaya is one such place, located directly opposite Wat Phutthaisawan. Its architecture—a blend of modern and traditional design—along with its riverfront views, makes it a peaceful retreat after a day of temple-hopping. Dining in Ayutthaya should definitely include trying some local delicacies; the Ban U Thong Restaurant offers traditional Thai dishes with a focus on fresh, local ingredients and is a favorite among both locals and tourists.

Visiting Ayutthaya is not just about exploring the physical remnants of its temples and palaces; it's about reimagining the splendor of an ancient city that was once home to Siamese kings, bustling markets, and foreign diplomats from far and wide. It's about sitting quietly by the ruins at dusk, feeling the cool stone under your hand, and hearing the echo of monks' chants in the distance—a journey through ancient kingdoms that leaves a lasting impression on your soul.

Sukhothai: Exploring Thailand's First Capital

Journeying through Thailand's historic heartland, Sukhothai, the first capital of the Kingdom of Siam, presents an awe-inspiring chapter of Thai heritage that spans back to the 13th century. This ancient city, whose name means "Dawn of Happiness," offers an evocative glimpse into Thailand's cultural dawn, revealing the origins of many aspects of Thai civilization that have shaped the nation's identity.

Located in the lower northern part of Thailand, approximately 427 kilometers from Bangkok, Sukhothai is accessible by road, air, and rail. The nearest airport is in Sukhothai itself, offering daily flights from Bangkok, making it a convenient entry point for those wanting to delve straight into the heart of Thai history. Alternatively, taking a train to the nearby city of Phitsanulok followed by a short bus ride to Sukhothai allows travelers to enjoy the scenic beauty of the rural Thai landscape.

Upon arrival, the vast Sukhothai Historical Park, a UNESCO World Heritage site, encapsulates the grandeur of this ancient city with its well-preserved monumental ruins. As you step into the historical park, the central area, with its impressive Royal Palace and the majestic Wat Mahathat, sets the stage for exploration. This temple, the largest in the complex, is surrounded by a moat and was the spiritual center of the kingdom, featuring a main stupa flanked by standing Buddha statues that catch the light of the morning sun in the most magical way.

Exploring further, the park's zones are dotted with various ruins, each telling its own story of a bygone era. The striking Buddha figures at Wat Si Chum, for example, have captivated visitors for centuries. Here, the monumental seated Buddha, peering through the narrow slit of its enclosing structure, offers a serene yet powerful image that remains etched in memory.

For those seeking deeper insights, the Ramkhamhaeng National Museum provides context to the ruins, displaying artifacts that range from intricate stonework to everyday items that paint a fuller picture of ancient Sukhothai life.

Accommodation in Sukhothai blends modern comfort with traditional Thai elements. The Legendha Sukhothai Resort is one such place, offering Thai-style villas that provide a peaceful retreat just outside the historical park. Its tranquil setting and proximity to the ruins make it a perfect base for both relaxation and exploration.

Dining in Sukhothai also reflects its rich heritage, with local eateries around the historical park offering authentic Thai dishes, such as the famous Sukhothai noodles. These are a unique blend of rice noodles in a broth enriched with dark soy sauce, topped with lime, crushed peanuts, and dried shrimp, making a delightful lunch between temple visits.

Visiting Sukhothai is more than just a sightseeing experience; it's a journey back in time where every path and ruin has a story, offering a profound connection to Thailand's ancient traditions and spiritual serenity. Whether you're wandering amid the ruins at sunset or cycling through the quiet roads that connect the old city, Sukhothai offers a reflective escape into the origins of a culture that thrives to this day.

Koh Samui and Beyond: Island Secrets

Koh Samui, a jewel in the Gulf of Thailand, is celebrated not only for its coconut-fringed beaches and lush mountainous rainforest but also for its less explored sister islands, which offer a serene escape from the more touristic scenes. Embarking on a journey to Koh Samui and beyond unveils a treasure trove of hidden gems, each with unique characteristics that captivate and enchant those who venture here.

Located about 35 kilometers off the east coast of Thailand, Koh Samui is accessible via a short flight from Bangkok,

Phuket, or Chiang Mai. For those preferring a scenic approach, ferries from Surat Thani on the mainland provide a picturesque passage across the blue waters of the Gulf, delivering travelers to this island paradise.

Upon arriving in Koh Samui, the diversity of experiences is profound. From the bustling beach scenes at Chaweng and Lamai to the more tranquil, untouched northern shores like Maenam and Bophut, the island caters to all preferences. Bophut, especially, is home to the Fisherman's Village, where old wooden Chinese shop-houses have been converted into chic boutiques, cozy cafes, and upscale restaurants, offering a blend of rustic charm and modern convenience.

Beyond Koh Samui, the neighboring islands beckon. Koh Phangan and Koh Tao are just a boat ride away, each island offering a distinct vibe. Koh Phangan, famous for its full moon parties, also holds secret spots like Than Sadet and Bottle Beach, secluded paradises that offer peace and privacy amidst nature's splendor. Meanwhile, Koh Tao, a haven for scuba divers, boasts some of the best dive sites in Southeast Asia with vibrant coral reefs and an abundance of marine life.

Exploring further, the Ang Thong National Marine Park, an archipelago of 42 islands, is an essential visit for anyone in this region. Accessible via organized tours from Koh Samui, these islands are virtually untouched by human development. Here, kayaking through the hidden lagoons or hiking up to viewpoint over the Emerald Lake on Koh Mae Ko provides an exhilarating connection with nature.

For accommodations, Koh Samui offers a range from the ultra-luxurious Four Seasons Resort Koh Samui, located on the secluded Laem Yai Bay, to the more quaint and charming Zazen Boutique Resort & Spa in Bophut, which provides a cozy, cultural experience with a beachfront setting. Dining on the island offers a similar variety, with high-end options like Dining on the Rocks at Six Senses Samui, where innovative dishes are served with stunning sea views, contrasting with local Thai eateries that offer authentic flavors in a more laid-back atmosphere.

The secret spots of Koh Samui and its surrounding islands offer a rich tapestry of experiences, from the decadent to the earthy, from the spiritual to the hedonistic. Whether you're sunbathing on a secluded beach, diving in crystal-clear waters, or indulging in gourmet cuisine with a view, the islands provide a profound sense of discovery and escape that resonates deeply with all who explore here. This corner of Thailand, with its hidden towns and secret spots, invites travelers to dig deeper, stay longer, and embrace the gentle pace of island life.

CHAPTER 10

ADVENTURES AND ACTIVITIES

Thailand, a land of endless adventure and cultural richness, invites every traveler to experience its diverse landscapes and vibrant traditions. From the lush jungles and soaring peaks of its northern regions to the crystal-clear waters and soft sands of its tropical islands, this country offers a bounty of activities that engage the body and elevate the spirit.

In this chapter, we will embark on a journey through Thailand's outdoor adventures. Imagine trekking through the dense foliage of Khao Sok National Park, where ancient rainforests echo with the calls of exotic wildlife, or scaling the heights of Doi Inthanon, Thailand's tallest peak, which offers breathtaking views and a refreshing escape from the tropical heat. Each national park and trekking route showcases the natural splendor of Thailand, offering opportunities for both the casual hiker and the seasoned trekker.

But the adventure doesn't end on land. Thailand's seas are a playground for water enthusiasts. Diving, snorkeling, and kayaking adventures await around islands like Koh Tao and Koh Phi Phi, where underwater life teems with colorful coral, majestic manta rays, and the elusive whale shark. Whether you're a beginner looking to get your feet wet in a diving course or an experienced diver aiming to explore hidden underwater caves, Thailand's waters promise thrilling encounters.

Beyond the physical thrills, Thailand's cultural pursuits offer a different kind of adventure. The country's rich history is displayed across countless temples, from the majestic ruins of Ayutthaya to the tranquil beauty of Chiang Mai's Wat Phra That Doi Suthep. Each site offers a window into the past and a chance to reflect on the spiritual and artistic achievements of the Thai people. The annual festivals, such as Songkran and Loy Krathong, invite visitors to immerse themselves in celebrations that are as meaningful as they are exuberant, filled with vibrant processions, traditional music, and community spirit.

Each corner of Thailand, from its bustling cities to the serene countryside, offers more than just activities—it offers gateways to new experiences. Whether you're paddling through the quiet waters of a secluded bay, uncovering the secrets of a historic temple, or joining in a local festival, you're not just observing; you're actively participating in Thailand's living story. These adventures and activities are not just about discovering Thailand—they're about discovering yourself amidst the wonders of a truly captivating land.

Outdoor Adventures: National Parks and Jungle Treks

Exploring the national parks and embarking on jungle treks in Thailand offers a profound way to connect with the country's lush landscapes and incredible biodiversity. From the dense rainforests in the south to the rugged mountains in the north, Thailand's national parks are sanctuaries of natural beauty and adventure, each providing a unique experience that draws travelers deeper into the wild heart of this vibrant nation.

One of the most unforgettable experiences I've had was trekking through Khao Sok National Park. Located in southern Thailand, this ancient rainforest is older and more diverse than the Amazon. Trekking through Khao Sok is like stepping into a prehistoric world where towering limestone karsts rise dramatically from the thick canopy, and the air is alive with the calls of gibbons and hornbills. The trails here range from gentle walks to rigorous hikes that lead to hidden waterfalls and secluded caves. Exploring this park, you can't help but feel a sense of awe at the sheer scale of nature's majesty.

Another must-visit for outdoor enthusiasts is Doi Inthanon National Park in the northern province of Chiang Mai. Known as the "roof of Thailand," it houses the country's highest peak. The paths here wind through lush montane forests and past cascading waterfalls, each turn and climb offering panoramic views that stretch out over the horizon. The park is also a haven for bird watchers, with hundreds of species making it a vibrant place for those keen to spot some of Thailand's most exotic birds in their natural habitat.

For those looking to combine physical challenge with cultural insights, the trek to Doi Suthep-Pui National Park, also in Chiang Mai, is perfect. The trek can be strenuous but rewarding, leading adventurers past remote hill tribe villages and to the sacred Wat Phra That Doi Suthep Temple. The temple sits atop the mountain, offering serene views and a peaceful atmosphere that invites reflection.

Jungle trekking in Thailand isn't just about the physical journey; it's about the stories and secrets of the landscape. Each park and trail has its own history, whether it's a path used by local tribes for centuries or a natural site believed to house spirits and gods. Trekking here allows you to not only see the sights but also immerse yourself in the stories woven into the very fabric of Thailand's natural heritage.

Accommodation options near these parks vary, from rustic bungalows at Khao Sok Riverside Cottages where you fall asleep to the sounds of the jungle, to the more luxurious Inthanon Highland Resort near Doi Inthanon, which offers comfort after a long day's hike.

Whether you're a seasoned trekker or a casual hiker, Thailand's national parks and jungle treks provide an escape into some of the world's most enchanting landscapes. These adventures are more than just walks or hikes; they are opportunities to engage with Thailand's wild beauty on a deeply personal level, creating memories that linger long after the journey ends.

Water Activities: Diving, Snorkeling, and Kayaking

Diving into the crystal-clear waters of Thailand offers more than just a refreshing escape from the tropical heat; it's a plunge into a vibrant underwater world that ranks among the best diving destinations on the planet. From the coral gardens of the Andaman Sea to the hidden coves of the Gulf of Thailand, the country presents an array of water activities like diving, snorkeling, and kayaking that appeal to all levels of adventurers.

Having explored these waters myself, I can attest to the fact that the experience of snorkeling in the shallow reefs, diving among the wrecks, and kayaking through mangrove forests is as enriching as it is exciting. The warm waters teem with a bustling life-form diversity, making every dive and snorkel session a discovery of colorful fish, intricate coral formations, and the occasional, thrilling glimpse of larger marine life like sharks and rays.

Koh Tao, affectionately known as Turtle Island, is situated in the Gulf of Thailand and is renowned worldwide for its diving and snorkeling sites. It's a place where beginners can get their PADI certification and experienced divers can explore challenging sites like Chumphon Pinnacle, where whale sharks are often spotted. The underwater landscape here is mesmerizing, featuring massive granite boulders, vibrant corals, and a vast array of tropical fish.

For those inclined towards a quieter but equally spectacular experience, snorkeling around the Similan Islands offers a visual feast. The crystal-clear visibility and the abundance of sea life make it a paradise. The Similan Islands are a group of nine islands that are part of a marine national park where the biodiversity has been protected, resulting in pristine marine environments. Snorkeling here, you float above coral-lined underwater landscapes that burst with color and life, making it easy to lose track of time in this underwater wonderland.

Kayaking in Thailand presents a different type of water adventure, particularly around the spectacular limestone cliffs of Phang Nga Bay near Phuket and Krabi. Paddling through serene waters, exploring hidden bays and secret lagoons, and navigating around dramatic karsts that jut out of the sea provides a unique way to connect with Thailand's natural beauty. It's peaceful yet adventurous; each paddle stroke brings you closer to discovering quiet beaches and secluded spots away from the crowds.

One memorable place for these activities is near Koh Lipe, located in the southern part of the Andaman Sea. Known for its soft sandy beaches and natural coral reefs, the island is part of Tarutao National Marine Park, which ensures its aquatic surroundings remain unspoiled. The waters here are a diver's and snorkeler's haven, with visibility so clear you feel as if you're swimming in an aquarium.

For those looking to stay and explore, accommodations like the luxurious Sri Panwa in Phuket offer easy access to the water combined with world-class amenities. After a day spent underwater or paddling, dining at The Cove in Phuket provides the perfect end to the day with fresh, locally-sourced seafood that complements the oceanic experience.

Each water activity in Thailand is not just about the thrill or the visual spectacle; it's about a deeper engagement with nature that is both humbling and exhilarating. Whether you're looking up at the sun through a filtered lens of water, watching the light dance off the corals, or silently gliding through a mangrove forest, the water adventures here remind you of the beauty and vastness of the natural world, leaving a lasting impression that calls you back to these blue waters.

Cultural Pursuits: Temples, Festivals, and Museums

Immersing oneself in Thailand's cultural pursuits, from the awe-inspiring temples to the vibrant festivals and insightful museums, is to experience a profound connection with the country's rich heritage and traditions. These elements are not just attractions; they are the living heart of Thai culture, each offering a unique lens through which to view the past and present of this fascinating land.

Temples in Thailand are not only places of worship but also repositories of the nation's history and art. A visit to the majestic Wat Phra Kaew in Bangkok, which houses the revered Emerald Buddha, offers a glimpse into the spiritual devotion and exquisite craftsmanship that characterizes Thai culture. The temple's intricate murals and ornate architecture are mesmerizing. Venturing north to Chiang Mai, the tranquil Wat Phra That Doi Suthep perches on a mountain, offering panoramic views of the city below as well as a serene place to ponder the more contemplative aspects of Buddhism. Exploring these sacred spaces, one feels a deep sense of peace and reverence that pervades the air—almost palpable in its intensity.

Festivals in Thailand are a spectacular display of the country's love for celebration and tradition. The Songkran Festival, celebrated in April, is renowned for its exuberant water fights, a symbol of cleansing and renewal. Participating in Songkran, you experience firsthand the communal joy and familial bonds that are at the core of Thai society. Another captivating celebration is the Loy Krathong Festival, where thousands of lanterns float in the waterways and skies, creating a mesmerizing spectacle of light. The act of releasing a lantern symbolizes letting go of past grievances, a beautiful expression of forgiveness and new beginnings.

Museums across Thailand offer another facet of its cultural landscape. The Bangkok National Museum houses one of the largest collections of Thai art and artifacts in the country, providing insights into the royal lineage, religious practices, and the everyday lives of the Thai people throughout history. Meanwhile, in smaller towns like Lamphun, local museums offer a more intimate look at regional cultures and histories, often overlooked but richly rewarding in their storytelling.

Each visit to a temple, participation in a festival, or exploration of a museum is an opportunity to deepen one's understanding of Thailand's layered history and vibrant cultural tapestry. It's about standing beneath the golden spires of a temple as monks chant in the early morning; it's about laughing with locals as you dodge playful splashes of water during Songkran; it's about reflecting on the ancient artifacts that tell tales of yesteryears in quiet museum halls.

This journey through Thailand's cultural pursuits is more than just a touristic experience; it is an invitation to connect with the soul of the nation, offering moments of joy, reflection, and profound beauty that stay with you long after you've returned home.

CHAPTER 11

TAILORED TRAVEL EXPERIENCES

Thailand, a country celebrated not just for its scenic beauty and cultural richness but also for its ability to offer something special for every type of traveler, crafts each visit into a personalized adventure. Whether you're a solo explorer seeking the thrill of new discoveries, a couple on the lookout for a romantic getaway, a family in search of kid-friendly fun, or part of a larger group or a senior traveler prioritizing comfort and accessibility, Thailand's diverse offerings ensure that your travel experience is just as unique as your needs and desires.

For solo travelers, Thailand presents an exhilarating backdrop of freedom and discovery. From the bustling streets of Bangkok to the serene beaches of the south, the country is safe, welcoming, and incredibly easy to navigate. Here, you can delve into the depths of lush jungles, learn to cook Thai cuisine, or simply find yourself in the quiet of a Buddhist temple.

Couples will find that Thailand's picturesque landscapes and tranquil retreats offer the perfect setting for romance. Imagine dining by candlelight on a private beach in Krabi or taking a leisurely boat ride down the Chao Phraya River at sunset. Luxurious spas, secluded bungalows, and stunning natural beauty make it easy to find that special place where memories are made.

For families with kids, Thailand is a playground of experiences that cater to the young and the young at heart. The country's many water parks, interactive museums, and wildlife sanctuaries are not only enjoyable but also educational. Safe and full of convenient amenities, places like Chiang Mai's Elephant Nature Park or the imaginative children's museums in Bangkok are perfect for family outings.

Groups traveling together will find that coordinating trips in Thailand can be as exciting as it is seamless. Whether it's group diving trips in Koh Tao, trekking through the northern highlands, or enjoying the nightlife of Pattaya, Thailand offers a vast array of activities that can be enjoyed by all. With a little planning, even the largest parties can experience the joy of a well-organized adventure.

Lastly, for senior travelers, Thailand's hospitality includes a focus on comfort and accessibility. More relaxed cultural tours, river cruises, and beach resorts with first-class amenities ensure that senior visitors can explore and relax in comfort and style. The warmth of Thai hospitality means that needs are met with the utmost care and respect.

This chapter will guide you through these tailored travel experiences, providing you with the tools to carve out a personalized journey through Thailand. Whatever your style of travel, Thailand's rich tapestry of experiences promises to meet your wishes with open arms and unforgettable moments.

Solo Travelers: Freedom and Discovery

Traveling solo in Thailand is an exhilarating adventure that offers freedom, discovery, and the chance to immerse yourself fully in a new culture without constraints. The country's welcoming atmosphere, combined with its rich landscapes and abundant activities, makes it an ideal destination for those looking to venture on their own.

One of the greatest joys of solo travel in Thailand is the liberty to chart your own course. In Bangkok, you can weave through the bustling streets on a rented scooter, stop at any street food stall that catches your eye—perhaps for some savory Pad Thai or sweet mango sticky rice—and explore the grandeur of the Grand Palace without having to align your schedule with anyone else's. The city's extensive public transport system, including the BTS Skytrain and MRT, makes navigating this vibrant metropolis both simple and affordable.

Heading north to Chiang Mai, the experience shifts to a slower, more contemplative pace. Here, solo travelers can join meditation retreats in local monasteries, learning mindfulness meditation practices from seasoned monks. The serene surroundings and the focus on personal mental health are perfectly suited for introspective journeys that solo travel often inspires. Additionally, the city's night markets are a safe and lively place to stroll, offering everything from intricate handicrafts to live music, letting you mingle with both locals and other travelers in a casual setting.

For those drawn to nature, a solo trek in the northern jungles can be organized with local guides who provide insights not only into the flora and fauna but also into the local hill tribe cultures. Or, for a coastal retreat, the islands of the Andaman Sea like Koh Lanta offer a tranquil escape with long, sandy beaches perfect for days spent sunbathing, reading, and simply rejuvenating. The island's relaxed vibe is perfect for those who want to connect with other travelers or enjoy solitude in a beautiful setting.

Solo travel in Thailand also presents a unique opportunity to engage with the local culture deeply. Participating in a cooking class in a local's home in Phuket, for example, teaches you not just about Thai cuisine but also about the traditions and daily lives of the people. These experiences often lead to meaningful conversations and a true exchange of cultural insights, which are invaluable to any solo journey.

Safety, a prime concern for many solo travelers, is well addressed in Thailand. The locals are generally friendly and helpful, and the tourist police are responsive and accessible in main tourist areas. Common sense safety measures like guarding personal belongings and staying aware of your surroundings are, of course, recommended, as they would be anywhere in the world.

In essence, solo travel in Thailand is about embracing freedom—the freedom to explore at your own pace, to meet new people or enjoy solitude, and to engage with a culture rich in history and hospitality. Each city, each village, and each person has a story that, as a solo traveler, you have the unique opportunity to uncover and make part of your own travel story.

Couples: Romantic Retreats and Activities

Thailand, with its enchanting landscapes and soothing seascapes, offers couples a myriad of romantic retreats and activities that can transform a simple holiday into a memorable celebration of love. Whether it's walking hand-in-hand along a secluded beach under a starlit sky or indulging in a spa retreat that revitalizes both body and spirit, Thailand's romantic allure is unmistakable.

One of the most idyllic experiences for couples in Thailand is exploring the magical Phang Nga Bay. Located just north of Phuket, this bay is famous for its dramatic limestone cliffs jutting out of emerald green waters. Renting a private longtail boat allows couples to discover hidden lagoons and secluded caves at their own pace. The serenity and majestic beauty of this place, especially during the golden hours of sunrise or sunset, create an unforgettable backdrop for romance.

For those who enjoy a mix of adventure and relaxation, the mountainous landscape of Chiang Mai offers the perfect setting. Couples can embark on a tranquil hot air balloon ride at dawn, witnessing the picturesque scenes of lush countryside and distant temples slowly coming to life in the soft morning light. Following the flight, a visit to a local café that serves rich Thai coffee provides a cozy retreat to reflect on the morning's wonders.

Back in the bustling environment of Bangkok, romance can be found in the quieter corners of the city. An evening dinner cruise along the Chao Phraya River is a quintessential experience for couples. The warmth of the gentle breeze, the glittering reflections of the city lights on the water, and the soft melodies of live jazz set an intimate scene. Dining on exquisitely prepared Thai dishes while passing by iconic landmarks like the Grand Palace and Wat Arun adds a touch of historical enchantment to the night.

For couples seeking a more secluded escape, the island of Koh Lipe offers stunning white sandy beaches and clear turquoise waters that are perfect for days spent snorkeling and evenings enjoying beachside dinners. Resorts like the Serendipity Beach Resort offer private bungalows with ocean views, ensuring privacy and comfort. The island's relaxed vibe allows couples to unwind completely, enjoying each other's company in a paradise-like setting.

And of course, no romantic getaway to Thailand would be complete without indulging in a traditional Thai massage. For a truly luxurious experience, couples can book a session at one of the many high-end spas, such as those in the Mandarin Oriental Bangkok, where soothing treatments are designed to rejuvenate and relax, fostering a deep sense of shared well-being.

In every corner of Thailand, from the bustling alleys of Bangkok to the serene beaches of its southern islands, there are countless opportunities for couples to create new memories together. Whether it's through shared adventures in nature, relaxing spa days, or romantic meals under the stars, Thailand offers all the essential elements for a love story that will be treasured for years to come.

Families with Kids: Enjoyable and Safe Attractions

Traveling to Thailand with kids is an adventure that goes beyond the usual family holiday experience. Thailand's vibrant culture, friendly people, and a plethora of child-friendly activities ensure that families with kids not only have a relaxing vacation but also an enriching one.

One of the great joys of exploring Thailand with children is the abundance of natural attractions and wildlife experiences that are both safe and engaging for all ages. A visit to the Elephant Nature Park near Chiang Mai offers a remarkable opportunity for kids to learn about elephant conservation and interact with these majestic creatures in an ethical and respectful environment. The park's approach to tourism allows children to feed and observe elephants in their natural habitat, which is both educational and awe-inspiring.

For families seeking a blend of education and excitement, the many aquariums and ocean parks, such as Sea Life Bangkok Ocean World, located in the heart of Bangkok, provide an underwater adventure through giant glass tunnels where children can come face-to-face with sharks, rays, and colorful fish. It's a captivating experience that combines fun with a deeper understanding of marine life.

No family trip to Thailand would be complete without experiencing the country's stunning beaches. The beaches of Koh Samui and Phuket are particularly popular among families due to their clean, shallow waters and wide range of beachfront resorts that cater to families. These islands also offer a variety of water sports and other activities suitable for children, such as snorkeling, kite surfing, and beach games, which can keep the whole family entertained for hours.

For a more relaxed pace, the historical parks of Ayutthaya and Sukhothai offer a chance to immerse in Thailand's rich history through ruins that feel like giant outdoor museums. Kids can explore ancient temples and gigantic Buddha statues, ride bicycles through historical sites, and enjoy picnic lunches under the shade of huge trees—activities that combine learning with leisure.

Additionally, Thailand's numerous adventure parks and jungle safaris, such as those in Khao Yai National Park, offer families the thrill of spotting wildlife like monkeys, elephants, and various bird species in their natural environment. These parks often have guided tours that are tailored to be informative and suitable for children, making them both safe and enjoyable family outings.

Dining out with children in Thailand is also a breeze, with many Thai restaurants offering a welcoming atmosphere and child-friendly menus that introduce younger palates to Thai cuisine with less spice. Street food vendors are also a hit with kids, offering simple snacks like satay chicken, fresh fruit, and sweet pancakes.

Traveling through Thailand with your family, you witness the warmth of Thai hospitality, where children are cherished and welcomed warmly. This cultural embrace, combined with the country's diverse attractions, makes Thailand a perfect destination for families looking to share unforgettable experiences. Whether you're watching your kids play on a sun-soaked beach, learning about conservation, or discovering ancient cities, the memories made in Thailand will last a lifetime, bringing you closer together as a family.

Groups: Coordinating Larger Party Adventures

Traveling to Thailand with a larger group can turn a simple trip into an extraordinary adventure, filled with shared memories and unique experiences that cater to the interests of each group member. Whether you're organizing a family reunion, a corporate retreat, or a getaway with friends, Thailand's diversity offers a multitude of activities that can satisfy everyone in your party.

One of the key considerations for group travel is finding activities that keep everyone engaged. In Thailand, this is effortlessly achieved given the range of experiences available. For adventure seekers, group activities like ziplining through the rainforests of Chiang Mai or team-building exercises in the form of survival skills workshops in Khao Sok National Park offer thrilling experiences. These activities not only provide excitement but also strengthen bonds as participants encourage one another and work together to navigate the courses.

For those interested in a more laid-back experience, a private boat tour around the islands of Krabi or Phuket can be a perfect choice. Chartering a boat allows your group to explore hidden coves, snorkel in secluded spots, and even enjoy a sunset dinner on board. These private tours cater to your group's pace and preferences, making them a fantastic option for creating a day everyone will remember.

Cultural enthusiasts in your group will appreciate guided tours of Thailand's historic sites such as the grand palaces of Bangkok or the ancient ruins of Ayutthaya. These tours can be customized to include expert talks or workshops on Thai history and culture, adding an educational element to the sightseeing experience. Participating in a Thai cooking class or a traditional dance workshop can also be a delightful way for groups to immerse themselves in Thai culture and learn something new together.

When it comes to dining, Thailand's culinary scene is as diverse as it is palatable. For large groups, many restaurants offer private rooms or banquet-style dining where you can sample a variety of Thai dishes—from spicy curries to fresh seafood platters—in a setting that encourages conversation and camaraderie.

Accommodation also plays a crucial role in the success of a group trip. Thailand boasts a range of options that can accommodate large parties. Resorts often offer villas or adjoining rooms that provide both privacy and accessibility. Places like The Sarojin in Khao Lak or the Anantara Golden Triangle Elephant Camp & Resort in Chiang Rai provide luxurious settings with group-friendly amenities like large pools, spa facilities, and activity centers that can be booked for private events.

Logistically, coordinating transport for a larger group in Thailand is facilitated by ample options ranging from private bus hire to domestic flights that connect major and minor cities efficiently. Local travel agencies are also very experienced in managing group itineraries and can provide invaluable assistance in ensuring that logistics run smoothly.

Traveling as a group in Thailand means shared moments of discovery, joy, and adventure. It's about celebrating diversity in preferences and interests within the group and finding those special experiences in Thailand's rich tapestry that bring everyone together. From the bustling streets of Bangkok to the serene beaches of the southern coast, the landscapes of Thailand provide a stunning backdrop to any group adventure, ensuring that everyone leaves with stories to tell and memories to cherish.

Senior-Friendly Travel: Accessibility and Comfort

Traveling through Thailand in one's senior years can be a delightful and fulfilling experience, especially when accessibility and comfort are prioritized. Thailand's warmth extends beyond its climate; its hospitality industry is remarkably attuned to the needs of senior travelers, making it a wonderful destination for those seeking comfort without forgoing adventure.

For seniors, the key to a rewarding trip is finding activities that are low-impact yet culturally enriching. Many of Thailand's temples, such as the grand Wat Pho in Bangkok with its reclining Buddha, offer easy access with options for those who may find mobility a challenge. These sites often provide ramps and are manageable for those with walking aids or wheelchairs, allowing everyone the chance to appreciate the architectural magnificence and serene atmosphere.

River cruises in Bangkok are another excellent choice for senior travelers. These cruises on the Chao Phraya River are not only relaxing but also offer a panoramic view of the city's historic sites and modern skyline without the need for strenuous walking. Onboard, guests can enjoy a sumptuous meal and cultural performances, making for a memorable evening or afternoon that is as leisurely as it is enchanting.

The city of Chiang Mai is a haven for travelers who prefer a slower pace. The city's art and cultural center offers easy walks through markets like the Sunday Walking Street, where the products of local artisans are displayed. Here, one can browse traditional handicrafts, art, and jewelry, all the while immersed in the soft sounds of Northern Thai music performances lining the streets. The cafes and restaurants throughout the city also tend to be senior-friendly, with attentive service and comfortable seating arrangements.

For those seniors who enjoy nature but require accessible options, several of Thailand's botanical gardens and nature reserves, such as those in Doi Inthanon National Park, have well-paved pathways and viewing platforms that make it easy to enjoy Thailand's floral abundance and birdlife without venturing into rugged terrain. Guided tours, which can be arranged through most hotel concierges, often include transport directly from accommodations to the site, ensuring comfort throughout the trip.

Accommodations in Thailand are renowned for their hospitality and can offer specific amenities geared towards senior travelers. Many hotels and resorts provide rooms with accessibility features, such as grab bars in bathrooms and emergency call buttons. Luxury resorts, such as the Four Seasons Resort Chiang Mai, cater to a serene experience with spa treatments, meditation sessions, and yoga classes that focus on wellness and are suitable for all ages and abilities.

Dining out in Thailand can also be a great pleasure, as Thai cuisine is both vibrant and can be tailored to dietary needs. Most Thai restaurants are accommodating when it comes to customizing the spice level and ingredients, ensuring that meals are enjoyable without compromising on health.

In Thailand, senior travel is about experiencing the culture, enjoying the natural beauty, and doing so with ease and comfort. Whether it's exploring ancient temples, enjoying tranquil river cruises, or simply relaxing in the lush gardens of a resort, Thailand offers a gentle yet enriching travel experience that respects the needs of older adults, ensuring they leave with not just souvenirs, but also cherished memories.

CHAPTER 12

ITINERARIES

Welcome to the chapter where your Thai adventure begins to take shape—whether you're mapping out a quick, vibrant dash through the urban landscapes or planning an extensive exploration of lush jungles and serene beaches. This chapter on itineraries is designed to help you navigate through the richness of Thailand, tailoring your trip to fit both the length of your stay and your interests.

For those on a tight schedule, our Quick Highlights section provides options for one to three days that pack in must-see attractions and experiences. Whether it's exploring the grandeur of Bangkok's palaces and bustling markets, or a quick island hop to Phuket or Koh Samui, these itineraries are crafted to give you a taste of Thailand's diverse offerings in a short time.

If you have a week at your disposal, the One-Week Explorer itinerary allows you to dive deeper into specific regions of Thailand. This could mean immersing yourself in the cultural tapestry of the North with its ancient cities and hill tribes, or unwinding on the pristine beaches of the South, giving you enough time to explore and relax, all the while soaking in the local culture and cuisine.

For those fortunate to spend two weeks or more in this enchanting country, the possibilities expand significantly. Our extensive Thai journey itinerary facilitates a comprehensive exploration from the northern mountains to the southern coral reefs, with recommended stops at lesser-known gems that offer a more intimate look at Thailand's vast cultural and natural landscapes.

In addition to our tailored itineraries, Chapter 13 provides all the essential information you need to ensure your trip is as smooth as it is memorable. From practical advice on currency, banking, and tipping to insights on navigating the local internet and communication options, this guide is designed to help you manage every detail of your journey. You'll find tips on making the most of both free and paid tourist attractions, understanding the opening hours of major spots, and choosing between car rental and public transportation options.

This chapter also delves into guided tours versus self-guided explorations, offers advice for travelers with disabilities, and lists useful apps and websites that can enhance your travel experience. Before you depart, don't miss our departure checklist and customs regulations to ensure you have everything organized for your return.

By offering a combination of well-crafted itineraries and essential travel tips, this chapter aims to equip you with the knowledge and tools to create an unforgettable Thai adventure, tailored just for you. Whether you are a solo traveler looking for adventure, a couple in search of romance, or a family aiming to make the most out of your vacation, Thailand offers a plethora of experiences that are sure to leave you with cherished memories.

Quick Highlights: One to Three Days in Thailand

If you find yourself with just one to three days in Thailand, don't worry—there's a surprising amount you can see and do in a short period that will give you a tantalizing taste of what this vibrant country has to offer. From the bustling metropolis of Bangkok to the tranquil beaches of the southern islands, even a brief visit can be packed with unforgettable experiences.

Day 1: Explore Bangkok

Start your Thai adventure in Bangkok, a city that never sleeps and where tradition meets modernity. Begin your morning with a visit to the grandiose Grand Palace, the city's most famous landmark, which was the official residence of the Kings of Siam—and later Thailand—until 1925. The complex is awe-inspiring, with its intricate detail and beautiful architecture, housing the revered Emerald Buddha in Wat Phra Kaew.

Just a short tuk-tuk ride away is the vibrant Chatuchak Weekend Market, if your visit coincides with the weekend.

It's one of the largest markets in the world, where you can find anything from vintage clothing to local handicrafts, not to mention it's an excellent place for tasting street food like pad thai or mango sticky rice.

In the afternoon, take a relaxing boat ride on the Chao Phraya River, viewing iconic sights such as Wat Arun (Temple of Dawn) and the city skyline from a different perspective. This also offers a breezy escape from the bustling city streets.

Day 2: Day Trip to Ayutthaya
If you have a second day, consider a day trip to Ayutthaya, the ancient capital of Thailand, just an hour's drive from Bangkok. This UNESCO World Heritage site is home to magnificent ruins and temples spread out over the island city. You can explore the historical park by bike, making stops at major sites like Wat Phra Si Sanphet and Wat Mahathat, where you can see the famous Buddha head entwined within the roots of a tree.

Day 3: Relax on the Beach
For those who have a third day, head down to Pattaya or Hua Hin for a day of relaxation on the beach. Both can be reached within a couple of hours from Bangkok, offering beautiful beaches, luxury resorts, and various water activities. Pattaya also boasts the Sanctuary of Truth, a stunning all-wood structure filled with sculptures based on traditional Buddhist and Hindu motifs.

Culinary Delights

Throughout your stay, don't miss out on Thailand's famed culinary offerings. Bangkok alone has a dizzying array of dining options ranging from street food stalls to luxury restaurants that offer a broad spectrum of Thai and international cuisines. Trying local dishes such as som tam (spicy green papaya salad) and tom yum goong (spicy shrimp soup) will delight your taste buds and introduce you to the flavors of Thai cuisine.

Cultural Insights

Wherever you choose to go, make an effort to engage with locals and partake in everyday cultural experiences, whether it's watching monks receive alms in the early morning or simply chatting with vendors at a local market. These interactions often provide deeper insights into the Thai way of life and add enriching layers to your travel experience.

With this compact itinerary, even travelers pressed for time can enjoy a fulfilling experience in Thailand, making the most of every moment in this beautiful and dynamic country. Whether it's the historical richness, the bustling market scenes, or the serene beaches, a short trip can still encapsulate the essence of Thailand's diverse allure.

One-Week Explorer: Diving Deep into Regions

Spending a week in Thailand allows for a deeper exploration of its diverse regions, each offering distinct landscapes, cultures, and experiences. This extended time frame is perfect for delving into the unique aspects of a single region or experiencing a taste of several different areas, from the bustling streets of Bangkok to the tranquil beaches of the Southern islands or the culturally rich Northern provinces.

Exploring Northern Thailand: Chiang Mai and Surroundings Starting your week in Northern Thailand, particularly in Chiang Mai, provides a blend of adventure, culture, and relaxation. Known as the cultural heart of Thailand, Chiang Mai is surrounded by mountains and lush countryside. Spend a day visiting the historic temples like Wat Phra Singh and Wat Chedi Luang in the Old City. Take a cooking class to learn about Northern Thai cuisine — dishes like Khao Soi (curry noodle soup) that you won't find anywhere else in the country.

An excursion to the Elephant Nature Park, a sanctuary for rescued elephants, offers an ethical way to interact with Thailand's majestic national animal. Following this, a trip to the nearby Doi Inthanon National Park, home to the highest peak in Thailand, provides opportunities for hiking and visiting spectacular waterfalls and hill tribe villages.

Immersing in the Lush Landscapes of the East: Pattaya and Koh Chang

If you head to Eastern Thailand, Pattaya offers a lively beach scene with various water sports and vibrant nightlife. Just a few hours from Bangkok, it's a convenient coastal escape. For a more serene experience, extend your trip to Koh Chang, where you can enjoy quieter beaches, snorkeling, and diving in crystal clear waters, surrounded by lush, protected rainforest.

Southern Thailand: Island Hopping

No week in Thailand would be complete without exploring its famous islands. Phuket, the largest island, is a good starting point with its picturesque beaches and a wide array of activities. Take a boat tour to the stunning Phang Nga Bay, where limestone cliffs and emerald waters create breathtaking scenery. Continue to the Phi Phi Islands for some of the best snorkeling and diving experiences, with vibrant coral reefs and diverse marine life.

From Phi Phi, you can explore the less touristy but equally beautiful islands like Koh Lipe, known for its clear waters and peaceful beaches. Here, the pace slows, and you can truly unwind, enjoying the natural beauty and gentle rhythm of island life.

Cultural Deep Dive in Bangkok

End your week in Bangkok, a city that perfectly encapsulates the modern and traditional facets of Thai culture. Spend a day touring the grand palaces and temples, including the

Grand Palace and Wat Arun. Explore the canals of Thonburi on a long-tail boat, experiencing the quieter side of Bangkok life. As evening falls, visit Asiatique for a combination of shopping, dining, and entertainment along the riverside.

Throughout your stay, indulge in Thailand's renowned street food — from spicy papaya salad and grilled seafood to sweet mango sticky rice. Each region offers its specialties, allowing you to embark on a culinary journey alongside your travels.

A week in Thailand can be transformative, providing enough time to engage deeply with the places you visit. Whether it's the tranquility of the northern hills, the festive atmosphere of the beaches, or the bustling streets of Bangkok, each day is filled with new discoveries, rich flavors, and the warm hospitality of the Thai people. This journey not only broadens your horizons but also creates memories that enrich your understanding of this diverse and beautiful country.

Two Weeks or More: An Extensive Thai Journey

Embarking on an extensive journey through Thailand for two weeks or more offers an extraordinary opportunity to deeply connect with the varied landscapes and rich cultural tapestry of this vibrant country. With more time at your disposal, you can explore Thailand's famed cities, hidden gems, and remote corners, each providing unique insights and unforgettable experiences.

Starting in Bangkok: A Cultural Melting Pot

Begin your Thai odyssey in Bangkok, the bustling capital that never sleeps. Spend a few days here to soak in the grandeur of its royal palaces, like the Grand Palace and Wat Phra Kaew, and explore the city's vast network of canals which provide a glimpse into its past. The Chatuchak Weekend Market offers a vast array of goods and is a feast for the senses. For a taste of local life, take a boat down the Chao Phraya River and visit the vibrant flower market, Pak Khlong Talat, immersing yourself in the colors and fragrances of the city.

Venturing North to Chiang Mai and Chiang Rai
Travel north to Chiang Mai, a city that harmoniously blends modernity with ancient culture. Spend days exploring its historic Lanna temples, bustling street markets, and vibrant art scenes. Don't miss out on a visit to the Elephant Nature Park or a day trip to the picturesque Doi Inthanon National Park, known for its stunning waterfalls and trails.

Further north, Chiang Rai serves as a gateway to the Golden Triangle where Thailand, Laos, and Myanmar converge. Here, the slower pace of life and the lush landscapes offer a profound sense of tranquility. Visit the surreal White Temple (Wat Rong Khun) and the majestic Black House (Baan Dam

Museum) to explore the unique artistic heritage of this region.

Island Hopping in the South

From the north, head to Thailand's southern peninsula where a world of islands awaits. Phuket, Krabi, and Koh Samui are perfect bases for exploring smaller, less crowded islands. Go snorkeling in the Similan Islands, renowned for their crystal clear waters and rich marine life, or relax on the quiet beaches of Koh Lanta. Each island offers its unique charm and activities, from full moon parties on Koh Phangan to luxury resorts on Koh Phi Phi.

Exploring the Northeast: The Isan Region

If time permits, venture into the Isan region in the northeast. This area is less frequented by international tourists and offers a peek into rural Thai life. The ancient Khmer ruins at Phanom Rung and the vibrant silk-weaving village of Ban Pheu are highlights. The region's distinct cuisine, with dishes like som tam (spicy green papaya salad) and laab (spicy minced meat salad), will tantalize your taste buds.

Ending with Cultural Immersion

Wrap up your journey with a return to Bangkok or extend it to Pattaya for some leisure by the sea. Engage more deeply with the culture by participating in a meditation retreat, learning about Thai Buddhism, or taking a Thai cooking class to bring home not just memories but skills.

Throughout your travels in Thailand, take the time to engage with locals, learn a few phrases in Thai, and participate in local traditions. Whether it's through a village homestay, a fishing trip with locals, or attending a village festival, these interactions enrich your travel experience, offering deeper insights into the heart and soul of Thai culture.

This kind of extended trip allows you to not just see Thailand but to experience it fully, with each region offering new adventures, flavors, and learning opportunities. It's a journey that challenges and changes you, leaving you with a profound appreciation for Thailand's diverse beauty and the warmth of its people.

CHAPTER 13

ESSENTIAL INFORMATION

As you set your sights on a Thai adventure, having a grasp of the essential information can turn a good trip into a great one, ensuring that everything flows as smoothly as the Chao Phraya River through Bangkok. This chapter is your go-to guide for all the practical details you'll need to navigate Thailand confidently and comfortably.

From understanding the basics of currency, banking, and tipping to navigating Internet and communication across the country, we'll ensure you're well-prepared to handle financial transactions and stay connected, whether you're uploading a sunset photo from a Phuket beach or sending a quick update from a bustling street market in Chiang Mai.

We'll explore the best ways to experience Thailand's rich tapestry without breaking the bank, from free tourist attractions that offer a glimpse into Thailand's soul to paid attractions that warrant your Baht for a deeper dive into the culture. Knowing the opening hours for major attractions helps in planning your days efficiently, ensuring you don't miss out on anything from the Grand Palace's majestic architecture to the tranquil beauty of Ayutthaya's ruins.

Navigating Thailand means understanding your transport options. This section covers everything from car rentals and public transportation to the nuances of choosing between guided tours and self-guided explorations—each offering different perspectives of this diverse landscape. For those considering a self-driven adventure or the ease of hopping on a tour bus, we provide the insights necessary to choose what best suits your travel style.

Special considerations are not overlooked, as we discuss disability travel considerations to ensure that all travelers, regardless of physical ability, can enjoy Thailand's wonders. We'll also share our top picks for useful apps and websites to enhance your travel experience, from language translation to local restaurant reviews.

Finally, as your trip concludes, a departure checklist and customs regulations section will ensure that your return journey is as seamless as your arrival. Whether it's knowing what souvenirs are permitted through customs or how early you should arrive at the airport, we've got you covered.

This chapter isn't just a list of tips; it's a compilation of carefully curated advice drawn from personal experiences and thorough research, designed to empower you on your journey through Thailand. By the end, you'll not just be visiting Thailand; you'll be experiencing it with the confidence of someone who knows their way around.

Currency, Banking, and Tipping

Navigating the financial landscape of a new country can be as daunting as it is crucial, and Thailand is no exception. Understanding the basics of currency, banking, and tipping can significantly enhance your experience, allowing you to focus on the rich tapestry of sights rather than on monetary concerns.

Currency: In Thailand, the currency is the Thai Baht (THB), and it's available in both coins and banknotes. Coins come in denominations of 1, 2, 5, and 10 Baht, as well as 25 and 50 Satang (100 Satang equals 1 Baht). Banknotes are printed in denominations of 20, 50, 100, 500, and 1,000 Baht. The 20 Baht note is green, and it's a good one to keep handy for small purchases like street food or bus fares, as it's often hard to break larger notes in smaller establishments.

Banking: Thailand is well-equipped with ATMs and banks across the country, even in smaller towns. ATMs are the most convenient way to access your money, though they typically charge a withdrawal fee of about 220 Baht per transaction, which can add up. It's wise to either withdraw larger amounts less frequently or consider opening a Thai bank account if you're staying long-term. Major banks like Bangkok Bank, Kasikorn Bank, and Siam Commercial Bank have branches in most cities and tourist areas. These banks also offer currency exchange services with reasonable rates, so it's often more practical to exchange some money right at the bank if you're carrying cash in other currencies like USD or EUR.

Tipping: Tipping is not traditionally obligatory in Thailand, but it has become more customary as tourism has influenced local customs. In restaurants, it's common to leave small change or round up the bill, especially if the service was exceptional. A tip of 20 to 50 Baht is quite generous in most places. For more upscale restaurants, a tip of 10% of the bill can be a kind gesture if a service charge isn't already included. For other services such as taxis, tipping isn't expected, but drivers often appreciate it if you round up to the nearest 10 Baht. In spas or massage centers, a tip of around 50 to 100 Baht is typical and much appreciated by therapists.

Personal Experience: During my travels, I found that having a mix of small and larger bills helped immensely, especially when visiting local markets where electronic payments weren't an option. Learning to use local ATMs and keeping an eye on transaction fees helped manage my budget better, without needing to carry too much cash at once. At dining establishments, observing what locals did helped me understand tipping norms, and conversing with local staff often led to friendlier interactions and valuable local tips.

Navigating the currency, banking, and tipping landscape in Thailand doesn't have to be complicated. With a bit of preparation and understanding, you can traverse this beautiful country with ease, letting you dive deeper into its cultural offerings without worrying about the nitty-gritty of financial transactions. Whether you're bargaining at a bustling street market in Bangkok or settling your bill at a beachside resort in Phuket, a smooth transaction complements the rich travel experience that Thailand promises.

Internet, Communication, and Staying Connected

Staying connected in Thailand is surprisingly hassle-free, whether you're navigating the bustling streets of Bangkok, exploring the ancient ruins of Ayutthaya, or unwinding on the idyllic beaches of Koh Samui. Thailand's robust telecommunications infrastructure ensures that connectivity rarely becomes a barrier to communication or accessing information, making it easy to keep in touch with loved ones or manage work remotely while enjoying this beautiful country.

Internet Accessibility: Thailand offers excellent internet coverage, with Wi-Fi available in most hotels, cafes, and restaurants. Many of these places provide free Wi-Fi to customers, and the connectivity is generally reliable and fast, especially in major cities and tourist spots. For more remote areas, such as certain islands or rural northern regions, connectivity might not be as strong, but it's steadily improving.

For those who need constant internet access, purchasing a local SIM card is a practical option. Major Thai mobile operators like AIS, DTAC, and TrueMove offer tourist SIM cards that can be bought right at the airport or at any of their numerous outlets found in malls and towns. These SIM cards are affordable, with various data plans tailored to short-term or long-term stays. Setting up is straightforward, and the service staff at the counters are usually very helpful and fluent in English, ensuring you can quickly get connected without much fuss.

Mobile Connectivity: Thailand's mobile networks cover most areas of the country with 4G services, and 5G is rolling out in major cities. The reception is generally good, and using mobile data is an efficient way to stay connected if no Wi-Fi is available. For tourists, the cost of mobile data is quite reasonable. For instance, a typical plan might offer several gigabytes of data for just a couple of dollars, making it easy to use maps, travel apps, or social media on the go.

Communication Tips: When it comes to keeping in touch, most travelers in Thailand use popular messaging apps like WhatsApp, Messenger, and Line. Line is particularly popular among locals, and you may find that even small businesses prefer to communicate through it. For international calls, apps like Skype or FaceTime are convenient and cost-effective, especially if you are connected to Wi-Fi.

During my travels in Thailand, I found it incredibly beneficial to have a local SIM card. Not only did it allow me to navigate using Google Maps, but it also came in handy for booking rides via Grab (a popular ride-hailing app in Southeast Asia) or for instant translations in more off-the-beaten-path locations where English was not widely spoken.

Practical Advice: If you plan on driving or venturing into remote areas, consider downloading offline maps or travel guides to ensure you always have access to necessary navigation tools. Additionally, keep your devices charged; carrying a portable power bank can be a lifesaver, especially during long day trips where power outlets might not be readily available.

Staying connected in Thailand is easy and can enhance your travel experience significantly. With a little preparation, such as securing a local SIM card and knowing where free Wi-Fi is available, you can explore this captivating country with confidence and ease. Whether you're sharing photos of stunning Thai landscapes or calling home with updates of your adventures, Thailand's connectivity ensures you can stay in the loop no matter where your travels take you.

Free Tourist Attractions

Exploring Thailand doesn't always have to come with a hefty price tag. In fact, some of the most enriching experiences in this vibrant country come free of charge. From historical sites to natural wonders, there's a wealth of attractions that you can enjoy without spending a single baht. Let me guide you through some of Thailand's best free tourist attractions, each offering its unique charm and historical significance.

Bangkok's Historic Temples and Parks

In the heart of Bangkok, amidst the skyscrapers and bustling city life, lie several serene parks and stunning temples that are open to the public at no cost. Lumpini Park, with its expansive green spaces, large ponds, and paths lined with tropical trees, offers a peaceful escape from the city's chaos. Here, you can witness local life through the lens of morning Tai Chi sessions, leisurely afternoon strolls, and vibrant evening aerobics classes. While most of Bangkok's major temples have an entry fee, you can visit some of the smaller temples like Wat Intharawihan for free. This temple houses a towering 32-meter high standing Buddha, a sight that truly captures the spiritual essence of Thailand.

Historical Sites in Ayutthaya

Just a short train ride from Bangkok lies the ancient city of Ayutthaya, a UNESCO World Heritage Site. The historical park here is dotted with ruins of temples and palaces which you can explore without any cost. The hauntingly beautiful remains of Wat Mahathat, where a Buddha's head entwined in the roots of a tree can be seen, is one of the most photographed sites in the city. Biking through these ruins, you get a tangible sense of the grandeur of the former Siamese capital.

Chiang Mai's Cultural Offerings

In Chiang Mai, the cultural heart of Northern Thailand, many of the smaller temples do not charge entry fees. Temples like Wat Phan Tao, made entirely of wood, and located next to the more famous Wat Chedi Luang, offer a glimpse into the Lanna architectural style and are perfect for quiet reflection. The city also hosts several seasonal festivals such as the Loi Krathong (Festival of Lights), where you can enjoy festivities without any charges. The vibrant parades, the launching of lanterns, and the decoration of the Ping River are experiences that are as enriching as they are picturesque.

Beaches and Natural Attractions

Thailand's stunning beaches are mostly free to explore. Whether it's the popular shores of Phuket and Koh Samui or the more secluded beaches of Koh Lanta and Koh Chang, the natural beauty of these places is available to all. Apart from sunbathing and swimming, you can enjoy vibrant sunsets and casual beach games here. In addition to beaches, visiting national parks such as Khao Sok National Park can be free, provided you stick to the certain areas that do not require a guide or an entrance fee. Here, the lush jungles and the chance to see wildlife in their natural habitat make for a thrilling adventure.

Market Explorations

Visiting local markets, like the Chatuchak Weekend Market in Bangkok or the Sunday Walking Street in Chiang Mai, doesn't cost a dime unless you choose to buy something. These markets are not only places to shop but also cultural venues where you can taste local street food, enjoy live music, and observe local crafts at no additional cost.

Through these experiences, Thailand reveals itself not just as a destination to visit, but a place to connect deeply with history, culture, and nature. The accessibility of these free attractions makes Thailand a wonderfully inclusive destination, ensuring that every traveler can experience its richness, regardless of budget.

Paid Tourist Attractions

While Thailand is renowned for its multitude of free attractions, some of its most unforgettable experiences do come with a price tag. These paid tourist attractions are well worth the investment, offering organized, comprehensive access to some of Thailand's most iconic and awe-inspiring sights. From historical complexes to thrilling adventure parks, these attractions provide a deeper dive into the rich tapestry of Thai culture and natural beauty.

The Grand Palace, Bangkok

The Grand Palace in Bangkok is perhaps the most famous paid attraction in Thailand. Located in the heart of the city, this dazzling complex of buildings was the official residence of the Kings of Siam (and later Thailand) from 1782 until 1925. The intricate detail and stunning architecture, especially of Wat Phra Kaew, which houses the Emerald Buddha, make it a must-visit. Entrance fees are around 500 Baht, which contributes to the preservation of this historic site. The palace is easily accessible by taxi, tuk-tuk, or riverboat, making it a convenient destination for travelers staying in Bangkok.

Ayutthaya Historical Park
Just an hour's drive north of Bangkok, the ancient city of Ayutthaya is a paid attraction that offers a poignant glimpse into Thailand's regal past. The park encompasses magnificent ruins of the old city, which was Thailand's capital from the 14th to 18th centuries. The entry fee to the park is modest, typically around 50 Baht for each major temple complex, and it's worth every satang for the chance to explore this UNESCO World Heritage Site. Bicycles and guided tours are available for a fee, offering a leisurely and informative way to see the extensive grounds.

Phi Phi Islands
Access to the stunning Phi Phi Islands usually comes with a fee, whether you pay for a boat tour from Phuket or Krabi or choose to stay directly on the islands. The iconic views of towering limestone cliffs and crystal-clear waters justify the cost, typically ranging from 400 to 500 Baht for a ferry transfer. Once there, you can enjoy snorkeling, diving, and sightseeing tours, which, while paid, provide access to some of the most exquisite marine environments in the world.

Chiang Mai Zoo and Aquarium

For families traveling in the north, the Chiang Mai Zoo and Aquarium offers a chance to see a wide variety of animals from around the world. The zoo is located on the outskirts of Chiang Mai city and is accessible by songthaew or tuk-tuk. It offers an engaging experience with an additional fee for special exhibits like the panda house. Prices are reasonable, and the expansive layout makes for a full day's exploration.

Similan Islands National Park

Located in the Andaman Sea, the Similan Islands are a group of islands known for the clearest of blue waters and spectacular diving. Access to the park is regulated by the Thai government to protect its fragile ecosystem, and there is an entry fee for visitors. The fee includes access to several islands and is often part of a guided tour, which can include diving, snorkeling, and meals. Getting there is typically arranged through tour operators in Phuket or Khao Lak, who offer packages including transfers by boat.

Paying for entry to Thailand's top attractions supports conservation efforts and the maintenance of these incredible sites. It also ensures that visitors can enjoy a high-quality experience, complete with safety measures and educational resources that enhance each visit. Whether it's exploring the regal history of the Grand Palace, diving in the pristine waters of the Phi Phi Islands, or walking through the ruins of Ayutthaya, these paid attractions provide depth and context to your Thai journey, enriching your understanding and appreciation of a country that offers endless surprises and delights.

Opening Hours for Major Attractions

Navigating the opening hours of major attractions in Thailand is crucial to planning an effective itinerary. Let me guide you through some practical tips and typical opening times so you can make the most of your visit to this vibrant country.

Bangkok's Grand Palace and Temples

One of Thailand's most famous landmarks, the Grand Palace in Bangkok, generally opens to the public from 8:30 AM to 3:30 PM daily. Adjacent to the Palace, Wat Phra Kaew (Temple of the Emerald Buddha) shares the same opening hours. Just across the river, Wat Arun (Temple of Dawn) welcomes visitors from 8:00 AM to 6:00 PM. If you're planning to visit these iconic sites, arriving early can help you avoid the crowds that swell by mid-morning. The temples are accessible by taxi, tuk-tuk, or boat, which provides a scenic approach along the Chao Phraya River.

Ayutthaya Historical Park

The ancient ruins of Ayutthaya, located about an hour's drive from Bangkok, are typically open from 8:00 AM to 6:00 PM. This UNESCO World Heritage Site offers a full day of exploration, so starting your visit early is advisable. The park's sprawling nature means you'll need a good amount of time to wander through the various temple complexes. You can reach Ayutthaya by train, bus, or car from Bangkok, with local tuk-tuks available at the site for getting around.

Chiang Mai's Doi Suthep

The mountain temple of Wat Phra That Doi Suthep, overlooking Chiang Mai, opens its gates from 6:00 AM to 6:00 PM. The site is busiest at sunset when both tourists and locals come to enjoy the stunning views over the city and the temple's golden spire. It's accessible via a winding mountain road, and songthaews (red trucks) regularly make the trip up from Chiang Mai city center.

Phuket's Big Buddha

This massive statue on a hilltop offers panoramic views and is open from 8:00 AM to 7:30 PM. There's no entrance fee, although donations are welcomed. Located on the island of Phuket, the Big Buddha can be reached by car or scooter, with the journey itself offering beautiful vistas along the way.

Pai Canyon

For those venturing into the northern region, Pai Canyon offers an adventurous escape with no entry fee and no strict hours, although it's best visited at sunrise or sunset for the most dramatic views and cooler temperatures. The canyon is just a short drive from the town of Pai, easily reached by motorbike, which is a popular rental option for tourists.

Understanding these timings and planning accordingly helps ensure that you can visit these magnificent sites without hassle. Early mornings or later in the evening are typically less crowded, providing a more intimate experience of Thailand's rich cultural offerings. Always check the latest information as opening hours can vary during national holidays or for special events. With a little planning, you can ensure your visits are not only enjoyable but also perfectly timed to capture the essence of each location.

Car Rental and Public Transportation

Navigating transportation in Thailand offers a mix of modern convenience and local flavor. Whether you're considering the independence of a rental car or the authenticity of public transport, understanding your options will greatly enhance your travel experience across this vibrant country.

Car Rental in Thailand

Renting a car in Thailand can be a fantastic way to see the country at your own pace, especially if you plan to explore remote areas not easily accessible by public transport. Major airports and city centers like Bangkok, Chiang Mai, and Phuket have a range of international and local rental agencies, including Budget, Avis, and Thai Rent A Car. You'll need an international driver's license alongside your national license to rent a car. Costs can vary, typically starting around $20 per day for a standard car, which is a cost-effective option if you're sharing the ride.

Driving in Thailand is on the left-hand side, and while the main highways are generally in good condition, smaller roads, especially in rural areas, can be challenging. Navigation can be tricky due to signage often being in Thai, so having a GPS or a good map app on your smartphone is crucial. Always have comprehensive insurance, as driving in Thailand can come with hazards, such as unpredictable traffic and occasionally lax adherence to road rules.

Public Transportation in Thailand
Public transportation in Thailand is incredibly diverse, ranging from modern skytrains in Bangkok to traditional tuk-tuks and colorful buses. In Bangkok, the BTS Skytrain and the MRT subway system provide efficient and affordable ways to get around the city, avoiding the notorious traffic jams. A rechargeable Rabbit Card, available at any BTS station, can be used to pay for rides on both the BTS and the MRT. Fares range from about $0.50 to $1.50, depending on the distance.

For intercity travel, trains are a scenic and economical choice. Thailand's railway network connects major cities with sleeper options available for long journeys, such as from Bangkok to Chiang Mai or the southern provinces. Train tickets are affordable, with second-class sleepers costing around $25-$30.

Buses in Thailand are ubiquitous and cover more routes than trains. Government-operated buses are reliable and run long distances, whereas local buses are an extremely cheap way to hop around town. For longer distances, VIP buses offer more comfort and amenities, including reclining seats and air conditioning, typically costing between $15 and $30 depending on the destination.

For a truly local experience, songthaews (converted pickup trucks with two bench seats) and motorbike taxis are common in both cities and the countryside. They're incredibly cheap, though prices should be agreed upon before the journey begins.

Luxury Accommodations as Transportation Hubs

While exploring Thailand, you might consider staying at luxury accommodations that provide not just comfort but also convenience in travel connectivity. For instance, the Mandarin Oriental in Bangkok, located at 48 Oriental Avenue, offers not only plush accommodations and world-class amenities but also easy access to the BTS Skytrain, helping guests navigate Bangkok's lively streets. You can contact them at +66 (2) 659 9000 or visit their website for reservations.

Navigating Thailand's transport options offers a chance to see the country through a local lens or with the comfort and flexibility of your own vehicle. Each mode of transportation provides a unique perspective of Thailand, from the bustling streets of Bangkok to the serene landscapes of the countryside, ensuring your travel experience is as rich and diverse as the country itself.

Guided Tours vs. Self-Guided Explorations

Deciding between guided tours and self-guided explorations in Thailand can shape your entire travel experience. Each approach offers unique advantages, depending on what you're looking to get out of your trip.

Guided Tours: Opting for guided tours can be a great choice if you prefer a structured and informative path through Thailand's rich cultural landscapes and bustling cities. These tours often come with expert guides who provide in-depth knowledge about the history and significance of each site. This is especially beneficial if you're visiting historical landmarks like the ancient ruins in Ayutthaya or the temple complexes in Chiang Mai, where historical context adds a rich layer to the experience.

Guided tours can also offer convenience as they handle all logistics, from transportation to entry fees and sometimes even meals. This can be particularly appealing for those who wish to avoid the hassle of planning every detail or are concerned about navigating language barriers. For example, many tour companies offer day trips from Bangkok to the floating markets and the Bridge on the River Kwai, providing not just transport but also insights into the historical and cultural significance of these sites.

However, guided tours can sometimes lack flexibility, requiring participants to adhere to a predetermined schedule and itinerary. This might mean less time to explore each location on your own or fewer opportunities to spontaneously discover hidden gems.

Self-Guided Explorations: On the other hand, self-guided explorations in Thailand offer total freedom and flexibility. Renting a scooter to roam the lush landscapes of Pai or taking a slow train through the scenic views of the northern provinces allows for a personal and intimate experience with the places you visit. You can decide where to go, what to eat, and how long to stay, tailoring the journey to your personal interests and pace.

Self-guided trips require more planning and a greater sense of adventure. You'll need to navigate local transportation systems like the BTS Skytrain in Bangkok or songthaews in rural areas. While this can be daunting, it also offers a deeper dive into Thai culture and the daily rhythms of local life.

For travelers who choose to go it alone, it's wise to equip yourself with a reliable travel guidebook, a good map app on your smartphone, and some basic Thai phrases to help navigate and negotiate as needed.

Luxury Hotels and Resorts: For those looking to blend guided or self-guided adventures with luxury accommodations, Bangkok offers exquisite options like the Mandarin Oriental, located at 48 Oriental Avenue. You can contact them at +66 (2) 659 9000 or visit their [website](https://www.mandarinoriental.com/bangkok). This historic hotel offers not just opulent rooms and suites but also a strategic starting point for both guided tours and independent excursions around the city. Prices range from $250 to over $1000 per night, offering a spectrum of experiences from high-end rooms to luxurious suites.

Whether you choose the structured support of a guided tour or the personal touch of a self-guided adventure, Thailand is a treasure trove of experiences waiting to be discovered. Each option offers different pathways into the heart of this vibrant country, and either can lead to unforgettable memories and stories to bring back home.

Disability Travel Considerations

Traveling with a disability in Thailand presents a mix of challenges and opportunities that require thoughtful preparation and an understanding of the local context. While Thailand's warm hospitality and scenic beauty are inviting to all, it's important for travelers with disabilities to plan ahead to ensure accessibility and comfort.

Accessibility in Major Cities and Tourist Areas: Thailand's major cities, especially Bangkok, Chiang Mai, and Phuket, are gradually improving in terms of accessibility. In Bangkok, many newer skytrain stations have elevators, and a growing number of public buildings and malls offer wheelchair ramps and accessible restrooms. However, sidewalks can be crowded and uneven, which might pose challenges for those using wheelchairs or walkers. When booking accommodations, it's advisable to inquire directly about specific accessibility needs, such as wheelchair-accessible rooms or shower facilities, as these can vary greatly from one hotel to another.

Transportation: Regarding transportation, the more modernized transport systems in Bangkok, such as the BTS (Skytrain) and MRT (Metro), are equipped with lifts and designated seating for those with disabilities. However, smaller towns and rural areas might not have the same level of accessibility. Taxis and some private hire vehicles can accommodate travelers with disabilities, but it's best to arrange these services ahead of time to ensure they can meet your specific requirements.

Attractions and Tours: Many of Thailand's popular tourist attractions, including temples, parks, and museums, are making efforts to be more accessible. Major sites like the

Grand Palace in Bangkok and the historical parks in Ayutthaya and Sukhothai offer accessible paths in many areas. Nonetheless, some older sites might still be challenging to navigate due to uneven surfaces and limited accessibility modifications. It's a good practice to check with tour operators and attractions ahead of your visit to confirm accessibility features and available accommodations.

Traveling in Less Touristed Areas: For those venturing off the beaten path, planning becomes even more critical. The charm of Thailand's smaller towns and the natural beauty of its remote islands are enticing, but accessibility in these areas can be limited. Engaging with local tour operators who specialize in accessible travel can provide bespoke services, including transport, accommodation, and personal assistance.

Tips for a Smooth Journey
1. Communication is Key: Always communicate your needs clearly with service providers, from hotels to tour companies. Most are willing to accommodate, but clear communication helps ensure the right measures are in place.
2. Travel Insurance: Ensure your travel insurance covers specific needs, including coverage for mobility aids and any potential medical needs while abroad.
3. Local Contacts: Having contacts within local disability organizations can provide a network of resources and advice that can be invaluable during your trip.

Personal Experience

During my travels, finding accessible options required a bit of research and reaching out to services beforehand. On one occasion, a hotel went out of its way to ensure a comfortable stay by providing a room close to the elevator with a modified bathroom setup. This proactive communication helped make the experience more enjoyable and less stressful.

Traveling with disabilities in Thailand is undoubtedly improving, but it still requires extra planning and awareness of your surroundings. The country's natural hospitality and willingness to help, however, can make for a warm and welcoming experience, ensuring that all travelers can enjoy the beauty and culture of this vibrant nation.

Useful Apps and Websites

Navigating Thailand can be a breeze with the right digital tools at your fingertips. Whether you're exploring bustling city streets, wandering ancient ruins, or seeking out the best street food, certain apps and websites can greatly enhance your travel experience. Here's a breakdown of some indispensable resources that every traveler to Thailand should consider.

Google Maps

An essential tool for any traveler, Google Maps is invaluable for getting around in Thailand. With detailed maps of even the most remote areas and real-time traffic updates, it can help you plan your journeys whether you're driving, walking, or using public transport. The app's feature that shows business hours and popular times for visiting establishments like restaurants and attractions is particularly useful.

Grab
The Southeast Asian equivalent of Uber, Grab is widely used across Thailand for both car rides and food deliveries. It's incredibly convenient for securing transportation, especially in larger cities like Bangkok and Chiang Mai where traffic can be daunting, and public transport may not cover every area you wish to explore. The app also offers an English interface, which simplifies communication and fare negotiation.

12Go Asia
For booking longer journeys across the country, 12Go Asia is a fantastic resource. This website aggregates tickets for buses, trains, ferries, and flights, allowing you to compare prices and schedules and book online. It's particularly handy for planning multi-leg trips around the country and is known for its reliable service and straightforward booking process.

ThaiFriendly
To meet locals and get insider tips directly from residents, ThaiFriendly can be an excellent platform. It's a dating and social networking site where travelers can connect with Thai

locals. Many users are keen to meet foreigners and often open up opportunities to experience local events, home dining, and personal tours.

LINE

LINE is the most popular messaging app in Thailand. It's often used for more than just chatting; businesses use it to communicate with customers, confirming bookings for tours, restaurants, or even accommodations. Having LINE can also help you stay connected with any local contacts you make.

Eatigo

For food enthusiasts looking to explore Thailand's vibrant culinary scene, Eatigo offers a platform to book tables at a wide range of restaurants with time-based discounts. Available in major cities like Bangkok, Pattaya, and Phuket, it's a great way to plan your meals ahead and save money without sacrificing quality.

XE Currency Converter

Keeping track of your spending is crucial, especially when dealing with a foreign currency. The XE Currency Converter app offers live exchange rates and can help you quickly convert prices into your home currency to understand exactly how much you're spending.

TripAdvisor and Lonely Planet

Both TripAdvisor and Lonely Planet offer extensive reviews and recommendations for every aspect of travel in Thailand, from hotels and restaurants to excursions and activities. They are excellent for initial trip planning and for adjusting your itinerary on the go.

Using these tools, I've managed my travels through Thailand with much more ease and efficiency. For instance, navigating the chaotic streets of Bangkok became less intimidating with Grab, and connecting with locals through ThaiFriendly enriched my travel experience with personal touches that I couldn't have planned for beforehand.

With the help of these apps and websites, even first-time visitors to Thailand can navigate the country like seasoned travelers, making the most of every moment in this beautiful and diverse nation.

Departure Checklist and Customs Regulations

Preparing for your departure from Thailand is as essential as planning your arrival. To ensure a smooth transition from this wonderful country back to your home, there are several key items and customs regulations to keep in mind. Let me walk you through a departure checklist and a brief overview of Thai customs regulations to help you avoid any last-minute hiccups.

Departure Checklist

Passport and Visa Check: Ensure your passport is valid for at least six months beyond your departure date and that you have all necessary visas for your next destination if required.

Flight Confirmations: Double-check your flight details. It's wise to confirm your booking and check-in online if possible to save time at the airport.

Accommodation and Transportation: Make sure you've settled all your hotel bills and arranged transportation to the airport. In cities like Bangkok or Chiang Mai, traffic can be unpredictable, so allow plenty of time to reach the airport.

Packing: Remember to pack according to the baggage weight limits provided by your airline to avoid extra charges. It's helpful to weigh your luggage beforehand.

Prohibited Items: Ensure that you do not pack any prohibited items in your carry-on or checked baggage. Commonly restricted items include flammable liquids, sharp objects, and some agricultural products.

Valuables and Electronics: Pack valuables and electronics in your carry-on. It's safer to keep these items with you to prevent loss or damage.

Medications: Carry a doctor's note for any prescribed medications. Keep these easily accessible if you need to show them at security checks.

Travel Insurance: Keep a copy of your travel insurance details handy, in case you need to provide proof at the airport or need assistance before leaving.

Thai Customs Regulations:
When leaving Thailand, you need to be aware of specific customs regulations that could impact what you can take out of the country:

Buddha Statues and Religious Artifacts: These items often have restrictions, especially if they are antique or culturally significant. It's generally required to have a permit from the Fine Arts Department to export such items legally.
Counterfeit Goods: Avoid purchasing counterfeit goods such as fake designer clothes, bags, and watches, as these can be confiscated by customs, and you may face fines.

Restrictions on Tobacco and Alcohol: There are limits to the amount of tobacco and alcohol you can take out of the country without paying additional duties. Generally, up to 200 cigarettes or 250 grams of tobacco and one liter of alcohol per person are allowed.

Cash Restrictions: If you are carrying more than 50,000 THB (approximately 1,500 USD) or equivalent in foreign currency, you must declare this amount at customs upon departure.

Each of these points ensures that you leave Thailand without any issues, having respected the local laws and customs. I remember meticulously checking my items during my last trip; having a checklist helped me ensure I wasn't carrying anything that could raise concerns or delay my departure. Being proactive about such preparations lets you enjoy your final moments in Thailand without stress, reflecting on the beautiful experiences and memories you've created.

CONCLUSION

As you close this guide, imagine yourself stepping into the vibrant heart of Thailand, a country that promises an array of unforgettable experiences. From the golden spires of ancient temples that reach towards the sky to the lush greenery of sprawling jungles and the pristine sands of tranquil beaches, Thailand offers a tapestry of adventures that cater to every interest and desire. Whether you're meandering through bustling market streets, sampling the fiery flavors of Thai cuisine, or finding peace amid the serene beauty of a remote island, the diversity of activities ensures your days can be as packed or relaxed as you wish.

This guide has equipped you with everything needed to navigate Thailand's rich landscapes and cultural tapestries. You've discovered the best spots for culinary delights, from street food vendors to high-end eateries, and explored the varied options for shopping, entertainment, and nightlife that can keep you buzzing from dusk till dawn. You've been introduced to the sanctuaries of wellness, the exhilaration of outdoor adventures, and the profound beauty of Thailand's heritage sites. Each page is designed to help you craft an itinerary that mirrors your personal travel dreams, making every moment of your stay as engaging and enriching as possible.

Now, it's time to turn those dreams into reality. Start planning your journey today to experience the warmth of

Thai hospitality, the excitement of its thriving cities, and the peacefulness of its scenic retreats. Let the memories you've yet to make motivate you to book that ticket, pack your bags, and embark on a journey that promises not just a getaway, but a profound exploration of culture, nature, and self.

Thailand waits to welcome you with open arms—to astonish, delight, and leave you with stories you'll treasure forever. Prepare to be captivated by every experience, from the moment you arrive to the instant you, albeit reluctantly, bid farewell. The adventures that await in Thailand are not just trips, but transformative journeys that will resonate with you long after you return home. So, take the leap and make your next travel experience not just a passage through places, but a journey into the heart of Thailand.

Printed in Great Britain
by Amazon

54784266R00096